Rationalism and Poetry
Giuseppe Terragni's
Asilo D'Infanzia Sant'Elia

Brian Delford Andrews

Culicidae
Architectural Press

Culicidae Architectural Press
an imprint of Culicidae Press, LLC
918 5TH ST
Ames, IA 50010
USA
www.culicidaearchitecturalpress.com
editor@culicidaepress.com
+1 (352) 388-3848
+1 (515) 462-0278

RATIONALISM AND POETRY:
GIUSEPPE TERRAGNI'S *ASILO D'INFANZIA SANT'ELIA*

2019 © Brian Delford Andrews

All rights reserved. No part of this work covered by the copyright here- on may be reproduced or used in any form or by any means—graphic, electronic, or mechanical, including photocopying, recording, taping, or information storage and retrieval systems—without written permis- sion of the publisher. The publisher makes no representation, express or implied, with regard of the accuracy of the information contained in this book and cannot accept any legal responsibility or liability for any errors or omissions that may be made.

ISBN: 978-1-68315-016-9

Edited by Joanne Drilling
Book layout and design by polytekton

This book is dedicated to James Connie Andrews and Constance Walker Andrews

I would like to thank the following people for their help and support: Elena Andrews, Elizabeth Kruse, James Carrico, Alexander Ford, and Amedeo Petrilli.

Table of Contents

Introduction   7

Modernism in Fascist Italy   13
Modernism in Europe   19
Germany   23
Biography   29
Influences   35
Influential Buildings   47
The *Asilo*   63
Conclusion   115

Bibliography   127

Figure 1: Southern Elevation and Entry of the Asilo

1

Introduction

Como's *Asilo D'Infanzia Sant'Elia* occupies a unique position in the *oeuvre* of Giuseppe Terragni. Executed between his two most celebrated works, the *Casa del Fascio* of 1932, and the *Casa Giuliani Frigerio* of 1939, Terragni was possibly at the apex of his architectural prowess, via imagination and creativity, at its execution. The building itself is a physical manifestation encompassing Terrangni's seminal ideas and theories on architecture and urbanism.

The *Asilo* was also the first building completed post-*Casa del Fascio* with Terragni credited as the sole architect. Aspects of the design can be traced back to his earlier ideals of classicism while foreshadowing more modern ideas evident in his later projects. It is worth noting that the *Asilo* was also designed during the most tranquil period of Terragni's all-too-short career, during a time when his military responsibilities of World War II were not yet as burdensome (as was the case during the completion of the *Casa Giuliani-Frigerio*), nor was he under the political microscope of the *Stile Littorio* (Fascist architectural authority), as was undoubtedly the case during the *Casa del Fascio* project.

The *Asilo*, a public nursery school, was a relatively modest project, situated in a working class quarter of Como, just south of the city walls. Its humble location alone rendered the project a departure from the conspicuously public site of the *Casa del Fascio*, located

Figure 2: Novocomum Apartment Building
(permission of Trevor Platt)

directly behind the Duomo in the center of town. One can only imagine the sense of intellectual freedom felt by Terragni after the intense pressure he undoubtedly endured during the *Casa del Fascio* project. This corresponding freedom is to a large extent what intrigues architectural scholars on multiple levels. No longer shackled to the stylistic patrimony of the city proper, as was the case during the design of the *Novocomum* apartment building as well as the *Albergo Terminus* hotel, Terragni was free to engage his forward thinking theories on architecture, essentially pioneering a more refined and clear vision.

It is also one of the few projects that utilize all of Terragni's architectural canons. It remains the only built project that is neither *a casa del fascio*, nor a tomb or residential project. The *Asilo* remains a building largely ignored by both the academy and the architecture profession. However, this humble yet monumental building holds

Figure 3. Panorama showing the Entry and the Kitchen wing to the west (permission of Trevor Platt)

within it a culmination of the lessons and ideas of one of the modern architectural masters of the twentieth century. Careful analysis of this building reveals moments where architecture and meaning come together with both subtlety and consequence.

The *Asilo D'Infanzia Sant'Elia* was not hampered by the ideas of the *Stile Littorio*, that plague so many early Italian Rationalist schemes, nor does it suffer from the excess so prevalent in contemporary

Figure 4: Piacentini, Palazzo di Giustizia, Milan, 1940

Figure 4: Piacentini, Palazzo di Giustizia, Milan, 1940

designs. This building represents an unadulterated intellectual exercise where construction, technique, and art are held in careful balance. Marcello Piacentini, the most powerful and influential of all the Italian Fascist architects, known best for the *Palazzo di Giustizia* in Milan and *La Sapienza University* of Rome, proposed dividing the built environment into one of two types.

The first type is clothed in 'underwear', referring to its need for rationalism and structure, and the other clothed in 'evening dress', based on primarily the use of sumptuous materiality. Terragni's *Asilo* maintains its own category, clothed in a simple white *pinafore*, a child's smock, similar to those once worn by the very students who have occupied its halls. This nursery school still appears as decidedly modern and relevant as the day it was completed.

2

Modernism in Fascist Italy

Arcitectura Casabella Debate: Two Types of Rationalism

Modernism in Italy during the 1930s came in essentially two different modes. The first being *Piacentini modernism*, after aforementioned Fascist darling Marcello Piacentini, whose ideas were a slight departure from the neo-classical ideals of the *Novecento Italiano* group (including Anselmo Bucci, Achille Funi, and Mario Sironi, among others). The second, encompassing the Rationalist ideology of Terragni, along with Gino Pollini, Adalberto Libera, Luigi Figni, and several other Italian architects, identified as *Gruppo 7*.

The first key difference between the ideals of Piacentini and Terragni was the geographical location of their respective camps. Terragni, being located in the north of Italy, was far more exposed to the modernist ideologies of Switzerland, Germany, and the rest of northern Europe. However, this simple point alone cannot account for the critical difference that we see between these two factions. *Gruppo 7* was, to a certain degree, removed from the epi-center of politics, and its distance from the grandeur of Roman tradition must not be discounted.

In reality, architects such as Terragni were far more aware and respectful of history than Le Corbusier and architects working in northern Europe. Still, it is generally assumed that Piacentini and his cohorts were propagating a modernist architecture heavily influenced by historic styles. Buildings such as those at *La Sapienza University* in Rome and *Stazione San Maria Novella* in Florence with their rationalistic characteristics are strong examples of Piacentini's particular approach. Countless examples of this typology are scattered throughout Italy.

Terragni, on the other hand, forced his architecture through alternate filters, such as typology, geometry, abstraction, and simplicity that were perhaps more severe than his southern counterparts. His *Casa del Fascio* in Como certainly was singular in its more nuanced references to Classicism in comparison to other buildings executed during the Fascist period.

Figure 1: Casa del Fascio, Terragni, Como 1936

Figure 2: Academy of Fencing, Morretti, Rome 1936 (Wikicommons)

It referenced history in a way that even the esteemed Le Corbusier would have struggled to achieve. As an Italian and Fascist, Terragni was concerned with venerating the history of the Italian people and their culture, particularly the glorification of Rome. However, it is clear that while these two modernist factions were operating simultaneously, neither camp had particularly harsh feelings in regards to the other. Piacentini did not perceive the modernism of Terragni's *Casa Del Fascio* in Como as a slight against his own more *Novecento* style. Perhaps this can be attributed to Benito Mussolini who, unlike Adolf Hitler, was more comfortable with modern architecture. An example can be seen in Luigi Moretti's glorious gymnasium (often referred to as Duce's Gym), or his Fencing Academy, both part of the latter's contributions to the *Foro Mussolini*, later known as the *Foro Italico*.

Both the Piacentini Modernists and *Gruppo 7* were more motivated by paying proper respect to Mussolini than to the perpetuation of a specific style of architecture. Nothing else can explain the pluralistic examples of Fascist architecture throughout Italy. This attitude, or lack thereof, towards the Rationalist style of Terragni, certainly allowed him to continue to practice without fear of reprisal. We cannot imagine a similar situation in the other Fascist state of Germany. Other architects in the north of Italy were following similar paths. Cesare Cattaneo and Pietro Lingeri, also satellite members of *Gruppo 7*, were actively utilizing the Rationalist style. Overall the Rationalists were motivated to produce a language of 'modernity' while simultaneously continuing a national character that was more palatable than the machine aesthetic.

The similarity in the *Novecento* and Rationalist styles was the core belief in history and typology. But the main departure surfaced with the *Novecento* proponents who viewed architecture as a self-referential practice, whereas Rationalists were constantly invoking ideas borrowed from other art forms. The Rationalists were more cognizant of the work of their colleagues' contributions, specifically Peter Behrens, Erich Mendelsohn, Ludwig Mies van der Rohe, and Le Corbusier. They were also mindful of revolutionary artists such as Pablo Picasso and Piet Mondrian as well as Dutch architects Gerrit Rietveld and Theo van Doesburg. Essentially the *avant-garde* in Italy was uncomfortably close to the *arriére-garde*. New and old ideas were constantly comingling.

This understanding and sense of compromise, perhaps seen as a negative among fanatical modernists such as Walter Gropius, allowed for two separate yet parallel camps to vibrantly co-exist and eventually produce some of the most remarkable architecture of the twentieth century.

3

Modernism in Europe

Northern Europe

Architectural Modernism flourished throughout Northern Europe during the early parts of the twentieth century, most notably in France, the Netherlands, Austria, and the Scandinavian countries. There were also substantial gains in Germany, so much so, that it deserves its own section (to follow). France, however, held the most prominent position within the remainder of Northern Europe. Architects such as August Perret began experimenting with concrete as a material and form-giver early in the 1900s and developed significant advances in the Modern movement

Perret's *Garage Ponthieu*, completed in 1905, explored the concrete frame not only as a structural system, but also a visible architectural language. This concrete frame building retained aspects of traditional architecture, such as symmetry, and various framing devices. But more importantly, a young Charles Eduoard Jeanneret-Gris (later known as Le Corbusier) worked in Perret's Parisian office during those early years, gleaning a great deal of knowledge from his forward-thinking employer. The media-savvy Le Corbusier would undoubtedly become the paramount figure of Modernism in the early twentieth century, and his work certainly had a profound effect on Guiseppe Terragni on various levels, particularly in regards to the design of housing projects.

The signature clean lines and snow white surfaces of early Le Corbusier villas are easy to spot and document as key influences of Terrangni's evolving Rationalism. Terragni used many of the same principles employed by Le Corbusier, especially proportional studies, but Terragni was slightly more overt in his use of typology and precedent than Le Corbusier. As an Italian, he placed more trust in historical reference than the Swiss-born Le Corbusier. Undoubtedly projects such as Le Corbusier's *Villa La Roche* and *Villa Stein*, referencing Pompeian housing and Palladio respectively, had a profound influence on the young Terragni.

Another movement that possibly captured the attention of the impressionable young Italian was *De Stijl*, a Flemish movement

Figure 1: Villa La Roche, Le Corbusier, Paris 1925 (Wikicommons)

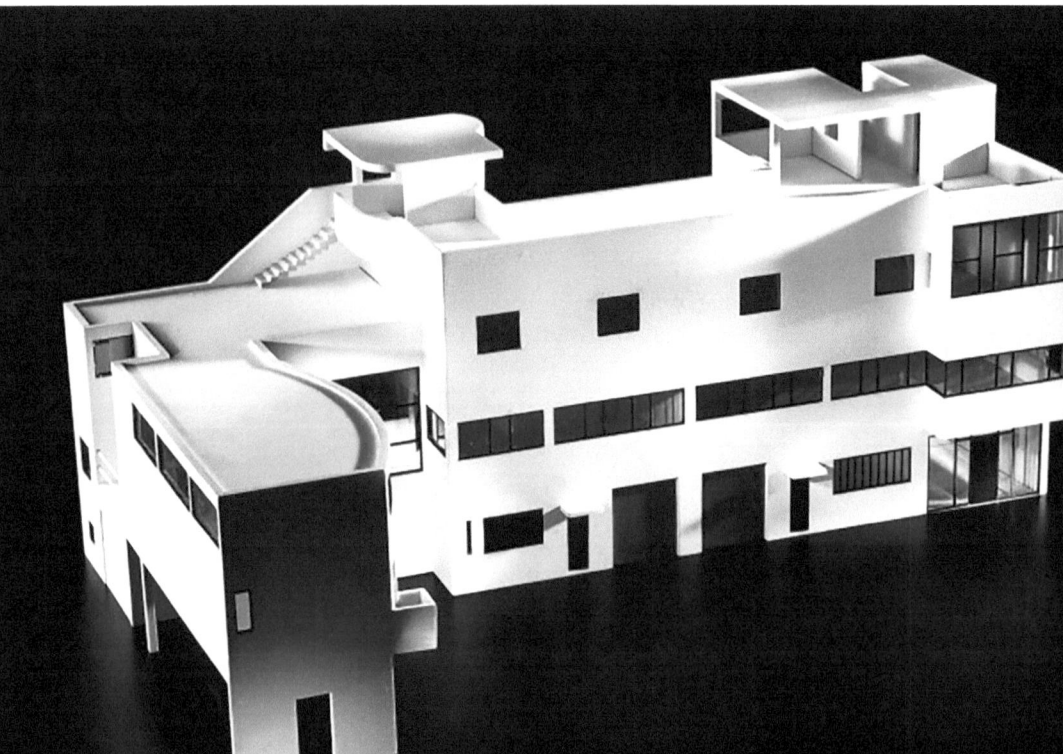

Figure 2: Villa Savoy, Le Corbusier, Poissy 1929 (Wikicommons)

Figure 3: Villa Stein, Le Corbusier, Garche, 1927 (Wikicommons)

that explored the relationship of architecture and art through color and visual composition. Terragni never used color extensively, however, he did use verticals and horizontals as primary composition devices in much of his architecture. He was far more abstract in his use of art as a catalyst than were the *De Stijl* architects. For example, the building-as-painting formula as seen in the Schröder House by Rietveld, was far too simple for Terragni's tastes, but he did utilize some of the spatial aspects indicative of *De Stijl*, particularly in the moveable walls of the *Asilo*. But ultimately Terragni achieved the reverse of *De Stijl* in that he moved from construction to abstraction.

Scandinavian contemporaries Gunnar Asplund and Alvar Aalto seem to have had little to no effect on Terragni and his peers practicing in Italy. At the same time the distance between the countries undoubtedly made it difficult to access visuals, let alone the true meaning behind their buildings. The same can be said for the Viennese master, Adolf Loos, who would have appealed to Terragni on a surface level, in that his buildings, on the exterior, were stripped to essentials and formed what would become the iconic "European cube."

4

Germany

Simultaneously in Germany, Modernism essentially revolved around three key figures: Peter Behrens, Walter Gropius, and Ludwig Mies van der Rohe. Gropius and Mies, both having worked in Behren's Berlin studio, would eventually flee Nazi Germany, settling in the United States. Gropius would become the guiding force of the architectural program at Harvard while Mies would do the same at the Illinois Institute of Technology. Le Corbusier was also a Behren's studio alum. Behrens's influence on these 'big three' of Modernism should not be underestimated.

Peter Behrens ushered in a very specific type of industrial aesthetic combining classical elements with a highly functional approach that he had honed from designing factories such as the IG Farben Höchst headquarters and the AEG Turbine factory. This minimalist approach was not without ties to the past, which might have indeed appealed to Terragni, however there is no hard and fast record of this. Still, it is important to note that Terragni was operating within a design field that had previously been tilled. Behrens's sublime factories are fraught with power and elegant simplicity, and are certainly forerunners of some of Terragni's later, more sophisticated works. Behrens's comprehensive approach to design (he is often considered the original industrial designer) undoubtedly influenced Terragni. The former concentrated on industrial objects such as fans, clocks, and teapots, while Terragni designed furniture.

An employee in Behrens's studio from 1908 to 1910, Walter Gropius (often considered the father of the *Bauhaus* movement), used lessons learned during his tenure at the elder's studio to forge his own methodology. Always striving forward, Gropius superceded classical formulas in the 1911 development of his design for the Fagus Shoe Factory in Alfeld, Germany.

At the client's behest, Gropius made a concerted effort to break from the past both in floor plan and materials. While he did remain tied to

Figure 1: AEG Factory, Behrens, Berlin, 1909 (Wikicommons)

brick as a building medium (at that time still the traditional choice for factories), he utilized a blond brick. As construction began in 1911, the brick completely transformed into a structural frame grid, as compared to solid walls. This reading was critical in terms of the perception of the building alone, but also in its significance to early modernism based on Sullivan's "form follows function."

It is also worth noting that Gropius managed to avoid a sense of overall symmetry in the Fagus Shoe Factory, a definite stylistic risk for his time. Despite these innovations, Gropius chose to embrace a classic design device—the Greek key—found in hallways and stairwells, thereby continuing the evolution of history as design methodology.

Figure 2: Fagus Shoe Factory, Gropius, Alfeld, 1913 (Wikicommons)

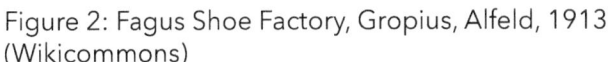

Once he was no longer tethered to the client's whim, Gropius returned to a classical model. His design for an ideal factory at the *Deutscher Werkbund* exhibition in Cologne in 1914 essentially upgraded an early Christian Church floorplan with a courtyard leading into a narthex, followed by a nave and a simulated transept. However it was clothed in a more industrially appropriate, factory-like aesthetic. It also referenced Behrens' 1909 AEG Turbine Factory which, some argue, was modeled after a Greek temple.

In 1925 Gropius began the design for his ultimate legacy—the *Bauhaus* School in Dessau—first utilizing what would eventually become his architectural 'calling card', the glass curtain wall. Hovering in front of the structural columns, this curtain of glass remains one of the most iconic elements of Modernism. In addition, Gropius was able to devise an overall plan that mirrored the abstract dynamism of the architecture school and its cutting edge curriculum in general. The *Bauhaus* School's use of stucco yielded an overall finish that was smooth and white, losing the traditional

Figure 3: Bauhaus, Gropius, Dessau, 1925 (Wikicommons)

modularity of brick and inspiring an aesthetic sense predicated on the clean lines of a non-materiality.

But Gropius was not the only former Behrens employee to strike out on his own to great effect. Ludwig Mies Van der Rohe was also faithful to his mentor's methodology, at least in his formative design years. His initial residential projects all consisted of designs based almost exclusively on historical models. However, due to a series of competitions in the early 1920s, Mies was able to shed this mantle and explore the emerging phenomenon of the glass skyscraper.

Around that same time, he worked on projects such as the overtly spare and earth-bound Wolf House and the seemingly weightless Barcelona Pavilion (completed with Lille Reich). Both projects allowed him to view, and then subsequently project, architecture through a more abstract lens while indulging in an almost sensual love of materials. The Barcelona Pavilion was an obvious influence

Figure 4: Barcelona Pavilion, Barcelona, 1929 (Wikicommons)

on Terragni. The graphic idea of the overlapping rectangles, which Terragni utilized later on many projects, including the *Danteum*, the *Asilo*, and the *Casa del Fascio*. Also evident was his love of materials and an obsession with glass and its ability to alter perception.

For the purpose of analyzing the influence these early Modernists had on Terragni, one must recognize that their genuine significance was the overall order and aesthetic sense of discipline, both of which were seen as de-facto elements in their work.

5

Biography

Giuseppe Terragni was born on April 18, 1904 in Meda, a small town located between Milan and Como. The youngest of four sons, he was dispatched to his mother's relatives at a fairly young age so he could attend primary and secondary school in Como. An eager student, he eventually graduated from Como's *Instituto Tecnico* in both physics and mathematics. But it was not until 1921 that Terragni set his course for architecture, enrolling in the prestigious Milanese *Scuola Superiore di Architectura Politecnico*.

Figure 1: Terragni in 1930 (Wikicommons)

The pedagogy at the *politecnico* was remarkably style-oriented at the time, requiring students to master mediaeval, gothic, and neo-classical forms of design. Included in the 2004 retrospective exhibition of Terragni's work was a note he sent his professor apologizing for an absence. His excuse? An impromptu trip to Rome to study classical Roman architecture.

While studying in Milan, Terragni befriended Pietro Lingeri, a fellow architect who would become a permanent fixture in his career. A skilled craftsman, Lingeri possessed a solid grasp of the mechanics of construction. His practical skill-set and grounded approach to architecture would allow Terragni to immerse himself in the more intellectual and theoretical aspects of the practice.

It was during his final year at the *politecnico* that Terragni began working as a member of *Gruppo 7*. Credited with importing architectural ideas across the Alpine region intact, the league consisted of Terragni, Luigi Figni, Guido Frette, Sebastiano Larco, Giuseppe Pagano, Gino Pollini, Carlo Enrico Rava, and Adalberto Libera. Collectively, they adopted the tenets of rationalism (such as the use of abstract and geometric terms in a constant alternating of solids and voids), and promoted the implementation of formal and functional research in Italian architecture. On the whole, the group was short-lived and the architects quickly went their separate ways.

As his graduation loomed in 1926, Terragni remained undecided as to whether he would pursue architecture or painting. Although he was an accomplished painter (very few works survive), he ultimately chose architecture. One year after graduation, he opened his own practice in Como at *Via Indipendenza* #23. It is both remarkable and telling that Terragni was able to successfully launch his own practice less than a year after finishing his studies, a feat that would be virtually impossible in today's economy.

The studio at *Via Indipendenza* also owed a large portion of its success to Terragni's faithful assistant, Luigi Zuccoli. Zuccoli worked tirelessly with Terragni on all the Como projects, including the *Casa del Fascio*, the *Asilo D'Infanzia Sant'Elia*, and the *Casa Giuliana-Frigeri*. Zuccoli went so far as to finish the final project, the *Giuliani-Frigero* apartments, while Terragni served on the eastern front as an artillery officer during World War II. While in the trenches, Terragni spent many spare moments sketching. He then mailed the drawings back to Zuccoli, who was able to translate them into designs for the final building.

If that was not hectic enough, it appears as though Terragni was running two distinct practices from 1927 through 1943. His Como practice with Zuccoli focused primarily on projects within the region, to which Zuccoli brought technical expertise. The second practice was run from Milan with Terragni's longtime friend and collaborator, Pietro Lingeri. The latter practice focused heavily on competitions, such as the *Palazzo Littorio* and the *Congressi,* and the numerous housing blocks, such as *Casa Rustici* and *Casa Comolli.*

It is worth noting that both Zuccoil and Lingeri effectively functioned as 'grounding foils' for Terragni's dynamic intellectual prowess at the respective studios.

Figure 2: Casa Giuliana Frigeri, Terragni, Como, 1940 (permission of Trevor Platt)

In the late 1920s, after joining the Fascist party, Terragni was joined at the Como studio by his brother, Attillio, an engineer. They worked tirelessly from his Como studio (it still stands today) until 1939, when Terragni was called to serve in Mussolini's army as an artillery officer. During the next three years Terragni was stationed at various locations in the Balkans, eventually ending up near Stalingrad, where he ordered artillery barrages against Russian teenage boys. Both physically and emotionally crippled by the violence, Terragni returned to Como a changed man. According to friends, gone was the gregarious, personable, and exuberant young man of the pre-war era. He remained haunted by the war and his role in human destruction for the rest of his days.

Figure 3: Casa Rustici, Terragni, Milan, 1935 (Wikicommons)

Terragni died on 19 July 1943, at the premature age of 39. While making himself a meal at his house, he realizied that something was amiss. He left food cooking on the stove and made his way to his fiancée's house. Reaching her apartment, he collapsed on the stairs, dying of an apparent embolism. Over the years there has been speculation as to whether or not Terragni took his own life, died of the embolism, or simply hit his head during the fall. Despite the actual cause of death, the world was robbed of one of the most promising young architectural minds of the twentieth century.

Figure 4: Casa Comolli, Milan, 1935 (Wikicommons)

6

Influences

When it comes to key influences, Michelangelo stands apart. Terragni's work referenced the Mannerist master on a number of projects and occasions. Case in point, the renovation of the *Hotel Metropole Suisse* in the center of Como demonstrates an overall debt to Michelangelo in the seeming malleability of Terragni's stonework.

Figure 1: Hotel Metropole Suisse, Como 1927

Monumentality, plasticity, and the play of flat and curved surfaces were elements of Michelangelo's *oeuvre* that influenced Terragni the most. The hotel project demonstrates Terragni's ability to work in surface, mass, and detail. The capitals and the subtle curved niches that contain urns all point back to Michelangelo.

Likewise, the *Monumento ai Caduti,* located in Erba, with its plastic stone forms and flowing stairs, also indicate an homage to Michelangelo. Another consequential reference to Michelangelo is apparent in the *Strecchini* and *Pirovano* twin tombs in Como's Monumental Cemetery. With their plasticity and classical references both of these elegant tombs are clear indications of Terragni's interest and knowledge of Michelangelo's work.

Figure 2: Monumento ai Caduti, Erba 1928

Another project, perhaps less obvious, is the *Casa del Fascio* in Como. Terragni's layering of the elevations recalls the ubiquitous layers of the twin facades on the Capitoline Hill in Rome. Terragni's ability to utilize classicism for inspiration, then reinterpret the respective ideas into his own more modern designs, is what ultimately separated him from many of his contemporaries.

A second, and almost opposing force on Terragni's approach was the Futurist Antonio Sant'Elia. Sant'Elia was an architect from Como who, despite very few completed works to his name, was known for his Futurist manifesto, bold designs, and sketches. The *Monumento di Caduti* in Como is, of course, the most direct influence.

Figure 3: The Stecchini and Pirovano Tombs in Como (by permission of Trevor Platt)

Figure 5: Pirovano Tomb, Como 1936 (by permission of Trevor Platt)

Figure 4: Stecchini Tomb, Como 1932 (by permission of Trevor Platt)

< Figure 6: Casa del Fascio, Como 1936

Figure 7: Capitoline Hill, Michelangelo 1546 (Wikicommons)

< Figure 8: Monumento ai Caduti, Como 1932

This act of bringing to life a perspective drawn by a fellow architect is a remarkable feat and speaks volumes about Terrragni's regard and respect for Sant'Elia. It is difficult to imagine one high-profile architect doing the same for another today.

It carries weight on other levels as well. Figuring out the structural and material requirements to fulfill such a task must have been daunting, at best. Terragni's ability to design an appropriate plan for the monument is also astounding. It illustrates a selflessness that is uncommon amongst architects, and especially architects that are as talented as Guiseppe Terragni.

The third, significant influence was the forward-thinking Le Corbusier. The International style, via Switzerland, was received by Terragni and *Gruppo 7* before any others in Italy. Ideas of form, principles, the effect of history, and Le Corbusier's five points all clearly dictated many of Terragni's early decisions. Terragni appears to have been consumed by Le Corbusier's work. He often referred to it by copying Le Corbusier's sketches for reference and also by putting together albums in the typical "Corbusian" method as he called it. This Le Corbusier influence is most pronounced in the small domestic structures executed by Terragni, such as the *Villa Bianca*, the *Casa del Floricoltare*, and most specifically the unbuilt Lakeside House. The *Casa Toinello* in Milan, despite the fact that it is an apartment building, clearly owes a great deal to Corbusier's *Maison Planeix*.

Figure 9: Villa Floricoltare, Como 1937
(by permission of Trevor Platt)

Figure 10: Casa Toinello, Milan 1933 (Wikicommons)

7

Influential Buildings

Casa del Fascio, Como 1932

Terragni's most significant building, the *Casa del Fascio* in Como, represents a culmination of many of his architectural ideas. What is perhaps most compelling draws on the fact that the *Casa del Fascio*, while considered Terragni's most overtly modern building, retains a very close relationship to his ideas of classicism and tradition.

Image 1: Casa del Fascio, Como 1936

The *Casa del Fascio* is clearly based on the classical Renaissance *palazzi* of Italy. The building's central interior space replaces the traditional courtyard in *palazzo* typology. Terragni skillfully manipulates the plan and section of the *Casa del Fascio* to serve the particular functions of the building. This central space (a pseudo-courtyard) demands a hierarchy that is paramount to the typical *palazzo* courtyard, as it is not open-air. Its covered, interior nature afforded greater flexibility and use.

Image 2: Plan, Casa del Fascio (the interior courtyard clearly ties the building to the typology of the Renaissance Palace)

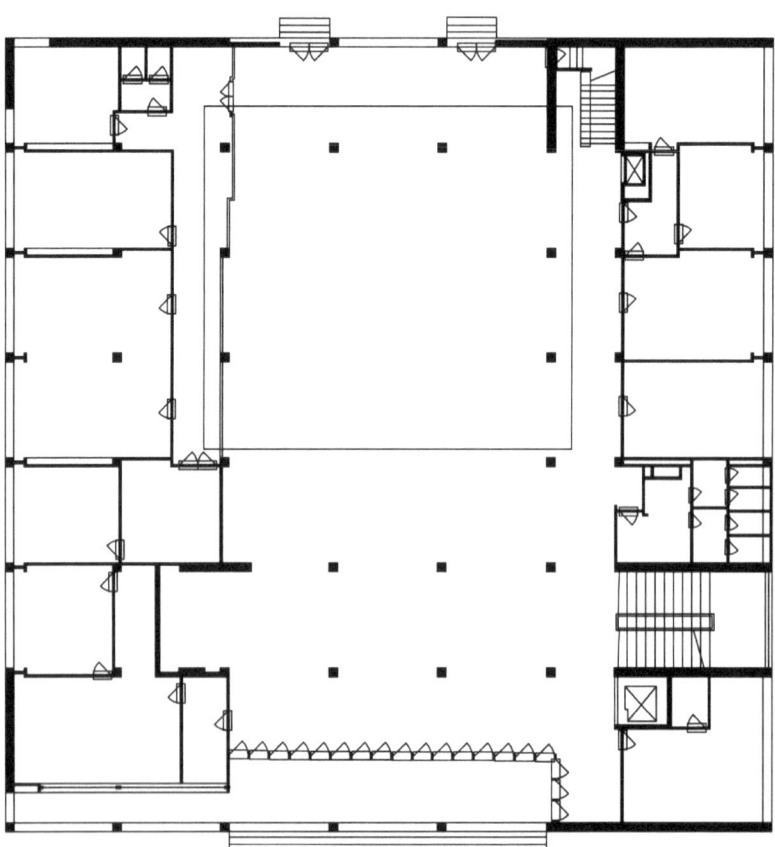

Image 3: Casa del Fascio, Interior of the central courtyard space

This explosion of space is a modern concept adopted and altered through the lens of tradition. Terragni's genius comes from his singular ability to manipulate and deploy this operation of using history as a method of furthering his modern ideas and forms. This type of operation occurs throughout his short career, resulting in numerous orchestrated overlays of history and invention.

These manipulations of form and meaning have resulted in an architecture that has remained timeless. Terrragni operates in a singular fashion that exploits a seemingly opposite condition that ultimately results in a new architectural reading. For example, a careful reading of the façade of the *Casa del Fascio*, results in an understanding that a shift has occurred whereby the traditional symmetry of a *palazzo* is challenged graphically to expose the functional layout of the building. The rooms that form the large right wall not only act as a large propaganda billboard, but also form the vestige of the 'Lictor's Tower', a traditional tower associated with urban culture and form in medieval Italian towns.

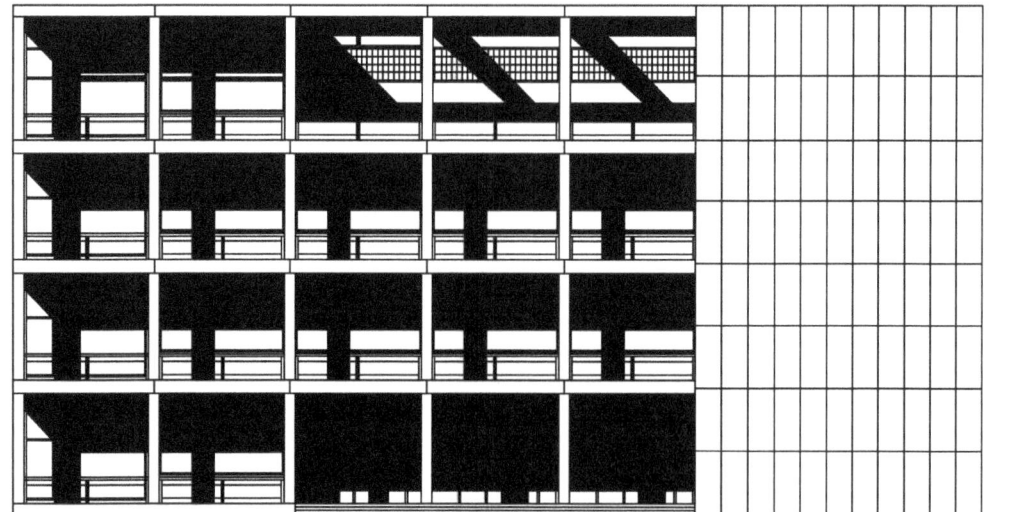

Image 4: Casa del Fascio, Façade (the large blank wall on the right sets off the symmetry and serves as the vestige of the Lictor Tower)

Image 5: Casa del Fascio, Façade

In reality, the spatial condition of the façade remains fairly symmetrical with the group of identical glass doors occupying the center of the composition. Manipulations such as this, whereby a functional gesture could be transformed into a formal gain, allowed Terragni to carefully negotiate his way through a complex series of forces and solutions.

Another opposite setup by Terragni takes the form of the material choice. The typical modern projects of the 1930s were very concerned with industrial materials and mass production. Projects by Le Corbusier and Gropius speak to this tradition. Terragni, as an architect from Como, with its particular *Comasco* (stone mason) traditions, understood and valued the character of the honorific material of white marble. As such he used it exclusively on the exterior of the building. The opposing force results in a modern building that is clad in a traditional material. The result of this choice provided a new reading and direction in modern architecture that is similar to the *Barcelona Pavilion* by Mies van der Rohe.

Image 6: Casa del Fascio, detail showing the white marble cladding

The proportions of the main façade are based on the square, or perhaps more precisely, on the half square. The plan of the building forms an approximate square, with the overall form taking the shape of a half cube. The diagonals of this half cube assist in the layout of the principal façade and generally dictate the placement of various elements. The overall grid of the façade is dictated by this action, however, this matrix is slightly manipulated in a way that ensures that it remains part of the *palazzo* tradition. The building is set on a small but critical base that extends the vertical dimension. This is coupled with the act of vertically extending the upper most module of the grid—resulting in the upper elements becoming perfect squares—which acts as a de-facto cornice. Terragni was undoubtedly aware that Michelangelo had executed a similar extension when he added the large cornice onto the *Palazzo Farnese* in Rome. Again, Terragni has brought together two opposing forces: the modern abstract grid with its inherent lack of hierarchy, and the base and cornice that place it within a traditional evolution.

Image 7: Casa del Fascio, detail showing the depth of the wall

Image 8: Casa del Fascio, detail showing the depth of the wall

The construction/structure of the *Casa del Fascio* is revealed through a grid system that is then altered to allow functional spaces to occur. This system is refined to such a degree that it is completely subsumed into the language of the building, resulting in a taut planar skin of white marble. This technique ultimately leads one to identify the building more as a solid figure that has in turn been carved out to reveal openings and spaces, rather than an additive strategy of construction. The exaggerated thickness of the walls and subsequent deep shadows around the openings contribute to this subtractive reading.

Even the siting of the building forms a series of opposites. The site was located adjacent to the historical center of Como, but more importantly, just outside the ancient city walls. The building is sited just to the right of the continuation of the axis extending from the *Duomo*. Originally Terragni had imagined a twin structure that would have been placed on either side of the axis, thereby achieving a balance without challenging the power of the church.

The *Casa del Fascio* immediately sets up a contrast to its surroundings in that the white marble is not consistent with the brown and grey colors of the traditional Como buildings that surround the site. Also the building is set back from the street edge, allowing the space for a *piazza* that was used during political rallies.

Image 9: Casa del Fascio, Site Plan (the building is situated off the axis of the Duomo, thereby not challenging the power of the church)

Image 10: Casa del Fascio. The white marble cube differs from its surroundings and utilizes the large piazza in front

Ultimately Terragni's white cubic structure serves as a lesson for architecture. It remains the quintessential Italian Rationalist building and has withstood the test of time. Its simplicity is rivaled only by its complexity. It utilizes both historic and contemporary ideas to form a union of parts into a pure whole.

The Palazzo Littorio, Solutions A and B

In 1934 Italian Architecture underwent an assessment of sorts through the *Palazzo Littorio* competitions. This hypothetical Roman building was to exemplify and embody the greatness of both Italy and Fascism. The building was to serve as a headquarters for the Italian Fascist Party, and as such required an architecture that represented aspirations of modern Italy while acknowledging the achievements of ancient Rome. The site for the project, considered extremely sensitive due to its immediate proximity to the newly excavated *Via dei Fori Imperiali*, was directly opposite the Basilica of Maxentius and Constantine. The site was specifically chosen so that the building could effectively act as a highly visible display of Italian culture.

Terragni headed a team of architects and designers that included Antonio Carminati, Pietro Lingeri, Ernesto Saliva, and Luigi Vietti as well as Marcello Mizzoli and Mario Sironi. Terragni and his team executed two separate schemes for this competition, often referred to as the historical scheme (A) and a modern scheme (B). In scheme A Terragni carefully employed shapes and forms that were reminiscent of the surrounding Roman ruins. His deliberate rendering of the site plan ensured that the size and density of the new walls (of the scheme) were almost indistinguishable from the surrounding ancient context. Terragni favored historical references, attaching a series of images to the competition boards that attempted to explain and illustrate the pertinent references to the design.

The scheme itself, as pointed out by Thomas Schumacher, owed a debt to Le Corbusier's Salvation Army building in Paris, in that the distribution of the elements on the site bore a resemblance to the Le Corbusier model. A large thin 'office block' was located on the northeast edge of the site, interrupted only by the *Sala dei 1000*. Placed along this dominant axis was also a collection of the hierarchical spaces associated with the program. A massive floating double wall, faced in porphyry stone, dominated the main façade of the complex. This wall was a clear reference to the Egyptian temple of *Isis in Philae*, which was one of the historic references that was on their presentation boards.

According to the renderings, inscribed into the stone of this wall, were the structural diagrams of the steel cables within the wall that allowed it to cantilever. This structural ornament was certainly unusual for Terragni, but perhaps it allowed him another method of exposing structure instead of the more common grid. A centered gap in the curved wall exposed a pulpit designed for Mussolini to speak to the masses. This enormous floating wall, comprised of a sacred material, was critical to the scheme. It managed to convey the theatre, the spectacle, the architectural power, and the historical context of the solution.

The larger parts of the program were all located in the foreground and were loosely placed along a series of axes and cross axes. Other than the north-facing glass façade of the office block, there seems to have been a conspicuous lack of windows, with Terragni relying instead on the recognition and power of the solid blocks and walls to convey the language of the scheme. Also missing is the 'Lictor's Tower' that was so common at the time.

The siting of the scheme was also significant in that the angle of the proposal in relation to the *Via dei Fori Imperiali* was exactly in opposition with that of the *Basilica Maxentius* across the street. Terragni's choice created a de facto composition between the *palazzo*, the basilica, and the colosseum.

Solution B also differed from solution A in that it placed a different emphasis on the building in terms of how it addressed the major street. A large, rather unrealistic, 230-meter cantilevered stone-faced wall, which apparently had no windows, confronted the passerby. The wall acted as a unifying element, ensuring scale and grandeur. Protruding through this horizontal wall was a large, more vertical element that the architects referred to as the "Lapis Niger", a clear reference to the origins of Rome itself.

Terragni's drawings and models give no clear indication as to the character of this wall in terms of its color. What is important is that, like the curved wall of scheme A, this element references history through materiality. The vertical element contained the rostrum for Mussolini, but at a much lower level.

Behind this hierarchical element Terragni placed the 'Shrine of the Fascist Revolution', an immense glass enclosure that reveals the architect's sensibility as a designer and the seeming intensification of his involvement in the second scheme. Ultimately, scheme B proved to be the preferred scheme, as it was more influential on the third and final scheme that was executed on a different site. The language of unification in the second scheme reveals the influence of Terragni as seen in other projects, such as the *Casa del Fascio*, the *Danteum,* and the *Asilo Sant'Elia*.

Palazzo Congressi

The *Palazzo Congressi* competition was perhaps the design that most clearly resembled the rest of Terragni's work. It utilized the structural matrix of the *Casa del Fascio*, as well as a more complex spatial scheme similar to the *Danteum*. The project was more clearly related to the confines of the *autarchia*, which specified using primarily Italian building materials. Gone are the unrealistic cantilevers of the *Palazzo Littorio* schemes. Instead we find a language more related to structure, and one more complex in terms of its layering and shifting ryhthms, resulting in an architecture that defies function and time.

The Danteum

The last project to discuss in terms of its relationship to the *Asilo* is Terragni's *Danteum*. As the name suggests, the Danteum is a project that celebrates the work of the Italian poet, Dante Alighieri. The *Danteum* represents Terragni at his most architecturally sophisticated moment. Due to its limited function, it allowed Terragni to experiment with pure ideas of space, materials, geometry, and form.

Using the narrative of 'The Divine Comedy', Terragni conceived a specific sequence that a visitor would follow through the complex. The project, which Terragni worked on with Lingeri, had a number of restrictions that in effect forced the constraints of the *autarchia*. This condition seemed to have aided Terragni with what most consider his masterpiece, compelling him to prioritize aesthetics over technology. The project utilized a number of motives that Terragni also deployed in the *Asilo*, such as the shifting rectangles, the extensive use of geometry, the practice of using architectural precedents, and the use of urban alignments as a way of achieving formal elements.

From a functional standpoint the project consisted of little more than a library, located on the lower level and coincidentally, off the sequence that was related to 'The Divine Comedy'. The project was to be located along the *Via dell'Impero*, essentially on the same site as the *Pallazzo Littorio* competition. Terragni recognized Dante as a symbol of Italian culture that connected ancient and current culture.

The entire building was angled to reflect the orientation of the *Basilica Maxentius*, located across the street. This achieved two objectives: It relates the *Danteum* to the Roman fabric both formally and intellectually; secondly, it allows the alignment of the *Danteum* to focus the view of the user towards the Colosseum as one enters the complex. This concept of 'the view' was critical in the *Danteum* and Terragni utilized it again in the *Asilo*. The visual connection was a method recognized by Terragni, and in a sense was a way of relating the project to the numerous urban views set in place by Pope Julius II during the Renaissance.

Terragni also sited the *Danteum* in such a way that its location related to the *Torre dei Conti*. Both the medieval tower and the *Danteum* appear to consist of similar geometries, and they both share an approximate angle in relation to the cardinal directions. In the siting of the *Danteum* Terragni has managed to reference both the Middle Ages and the Roman Empire.

The *autarchia* allowed Terragni to employ materiality that was familiar to the Roman urban context, such as travertine marble. It further illustrates how Terragni was capable of negotiating this landscape in a masterful and poignant way. An entry axis was utilized between the *Danteum* and the *Basilica Maxentius*, focusing towards the colosseum.

The visitors were then forced to turn around and continue along a very narrow, open-air corridor, essentially single file, thus allowing one to enter the *Danteum* completely alone. The visitors would then find themselves in the courtyard of the scheme. This almost square courtyard was adjacent to the hypostyle hall that represented the forest in the 'The Divine Comedy'. The visitors would wander through the forest of columns, ultimately arriving at a stair that would deliver them to the first of the critical rooms, the *Inferno*.

The *Inferno* space was dark and oppressive. It consisted of seven columns that each supported a square roof or platform. Each column and its square platform were independent of the others. There was a gap between the roof sections that allowed a small amount of light to penetrate into the otherwise dark interior. Each column is depressed slightly as one spirals towards the center. The columns spiral in the form of a nautilus and are based on the concept of the golden rectangle. This project, more than any other, illustrates Terragni's interest in geometry and proportion.

After moving through the *Inferno*, the visitors would follow a stair in the corner of the room that was slightly narrower than the previous stair and that subsequently led to *Pergatorio*. Here the room is based again on the same golden rectangle as the previous room, however it is reversed. Now there are seven square openings in the

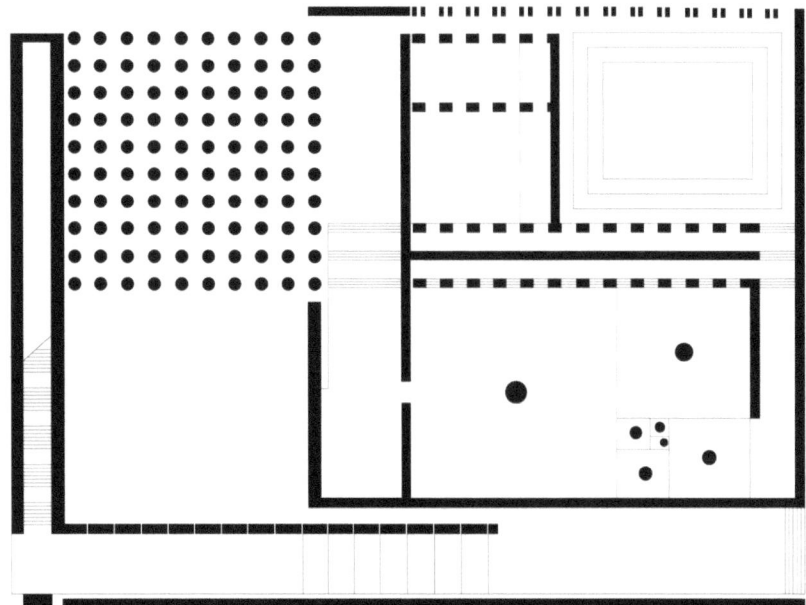

Image 11: The Danteum, Project, Terragni, Rome 1938, Plan

ceiling, allowing light to illuminate the room. Conversely, each platform ascends slightly, again forming the opposite of the *Inferno*.

After the *Pergatorio*, the visitors would ascend another, smaller stair to an antechamber. Here one would have the option of entering into the final main room, *Paradiso*, or to visit the *Empero*. The *Empero* was essentially a long corridor-like space that had a series of double columns running down its center. At the end of the space was a sculpture of an Eagle, which in Terragni's mind represented 'The Universal Roman Empire'.

The final room, *Paradiso*, took the form of 33 glass columns that supported an open framework of beams. Where each beam intersected the wall, there resulted in an opening that extended the entire height of the wall. Each column was independently supported by one of the columns of the forest below. This room, perhaps more than any other in the opus of Terragni, sums up his belief in narrative, form, geometry, and materiality as primary elements of architecture.

From the *Paradiso* one would finally exit out of the corner through the narrowest of gaps and descend down a long stair. That stair is aligned with a single solid block that is the element that starts the entire sequence. Terragni has effectively, brought the visitor on a sojourn, much like 'The Divine Comedy'. It was a hypothetical architectural journey that set a standard of monumentality and memory. If completed, it would have been the primary example of what Thomas Schumacher described as an absolute supra-historical architecture.

8

The *Asilo*

An *Asilo* seems to be a particular Italian institution. Loosely translated, it is a hybrid of a number of functions. It can best be described as a daycare/kindergarten combination that was originally meant to serve working-class families. It allowed parents to safely leave their young children while they both worked outside the home. It worked well as an institution within the Fascist ideology as well, in that both political and religious doctrine could be applied at a young age. The young children were cared for in a pseudo-educational format, whereby they were taught basic lessons. Beyond this, other functions were provided, such as dining and bathing.

One of the remarkable aspects of Guiseppe Terragni's *Asilo* extends from the concept that, despite the age of its occupants, he approached the project with the same clarity and intensity that he employed in the *Casa Del Fascio*. An *Asilo* was a building type that was often placed in an existing structure and was not considered a serious piece of Italy's architectural lexicon. Terragni exhibits a remarkable ability in his approach that elevates the building far above a daycare center and instead posits it as an environment that exhibits ideas about both Rationalism and Fascism.

The location of the *Asilo* in Como is significant in that, unlike some of Terragni's better known projects, it is removed from the historic city center. This physical distance probably allowed Terragni a freedom that he did not feel in the *Novo Como* housing or the *Casa Del Fascio*. The site was located in the working-class *Sant'Elia* district, and was directly across the street from a laundry facility.

The site itself took the shape of an irregular trapezoid that gave Terragni no clear direction in terms of a *parti* or a concept. Located on the corner of *Via Andrea Alciato* and *Via dei Mille*, the project essentially faces south and is situated on the south side of the city. The site is on a relatively flat plot. Immediately south of the site are the railroad tracks and the rising mountains where the *Castel Baradello* is situated. This relative remoteness and the relationship to the *Castel* were both critical in Terragni's site design decisions.

Image 1: Entry of the Asilo, showing the signage, the entry and the porch extending

Early Designs

The concept for the *Asilo* really began in 1932 when Terragni designed a school for 200 infants. This project, the *Clarita* nursery, was organized around a diagram that had four classrooms forming a linear block on one side and the assembly spaces grouped together in a slightly curved building that overlapped the classroom block. This overlap was rendered in a corner glass condition that exposed the major assembly space to the city.

The roof of the building was primarily to be used as exterior teaching and play space. Terragni also employed a ramp as the vertical circulation element that connected these levels. These lessons proved valuable in the *Asilo,* and Terragni improved them to solve many of the issues in the final design. This early project lacked the expressive quality of the layering and shifting that are so evident in the *Asilo*.

Second Design

There were actually a number of schemes that Terragni explored during the three years when the project was underway. They were all related in that they were centered on a three-sided courtyard with the rear portion open to a garden. A number of elements that were edited out during the process included a two-story portion that was located adjacent to what is now the kitchen.

The original scheme also contained only three classrooms, as compared to four in the final version. Other alterations involved the removal of an interior glassed-in courtyard, that took up much of what is now the play room, and finally a curved entrance canopy. Other minor changes included the removal of the showers and a series of catwalks. Finally, a number of offices, to be located above what are now the restrooms, were removed, although interestingly enough, the windows have survived.

Typology of the Asilo

The typology of the *Asilo* rests within two projects executed by Terragni. The first is the *Casa del Fascio*, with its articulated facades and ability to both represent construction as well as erosion. The attention to geometry as a design methodology and form maker extends into the *Asilo* and sets a standard that architects today can only hope to match. The *Casa del Fascio* sits as a complete object, developed on each façade, occupying the site in a logical way.

Spatially the interior courtyard, and its relationship to the *piazza*, separates it from other projects. The walls have deteriorated to the basic frame, allowing the light, activity, and views from the piazza to penetrate into the building itself. This sets the building apart from other Fascist architectural projects. It really represented a transparent house of government. The courtyard is exploited in a similar way as in the *Asilo*: It operates in an exclusively exterior condition but allows through, the use of transparency, the continuation of the interior collective. In the *Casa del Fascio* the courtyard

Image 2: Courtyard of the Asilo (permission of Trevor Platt)

is a space of gathering, whereas in the *Asilo* it is primarily a place of play and path. Terragni utilized this typology as a method to explore and solve numerous architectural problems.

In addition to the *Casa del Fascio*, Terragni had designed a library project in Lugano with Pietro Lingeri. It incorporated an aspect that became the critical element of the *Asilo*: the open courtyard. This horizontal explosion of space occurs in the library where Terragni split the program into two distinct bars and then allowed the

Image 3: Plan of the Asilo

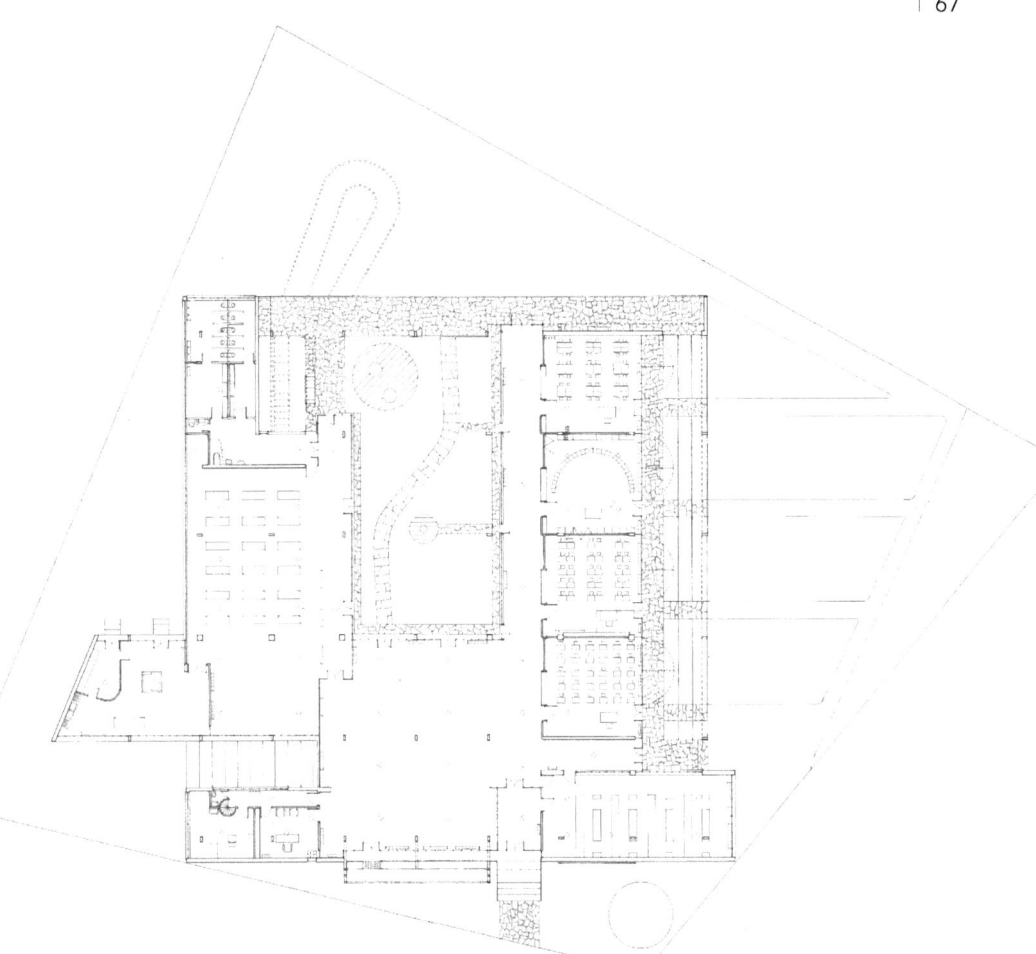

space between them to form the genesis of a courtyard to dematerialize, forming a U-shaped figure on one side. The project was located in an area that was not dense, thus allowing this type of freedom of plan. The library, however, was a multi-story complex that had none of the layering and freedom that Terragni was to explore in the *Asilo*.

Asilo Framework

The *Asilo* is based around a U-shaped figure that allows many of the manipulations to exist and to work together. This modified courtyard acted as a spatial explosion originating from the refectory and the indoor play space. The third wall is not rendered entirely in glass, but instead as a long horizontal window that mirrors the windows from the classrooms in the adjacent hallway.

To balance this horizontality, the vertical columns are projected out into the courtyard. This U-shape diagram forms the basic *parti* of

Image 4: View of the horizontal windows in the courtyard

the *Asilo*. It contains four disparate yet related elevations that correspond to four different functions. If visitors stand in this courtyard and look to the north, they are confronted with the freestanding column; as they turn to the right, the viewers are met with a series of columns that are displaced from the wall. As one continues turning, one finds a glass wall that has columns engaged. Finally, the fourth turn presents an entire glass wall where the columns appear to be absent. They are located behind the glass wall. This kind of Rationalism, combined with poetry, placed Terragni amongst the best of his genre.

Image 5: View of the columns extending out into the courtyard

Image 6: One wall of the courtyard with the columns exposed

Image 7: One wall of the courtyard with the columns hidden behind glass

Image 8: One wall of the courtyard with the columns engaged within the glass wall

Image 9: One wall of the courtyard with the columns completely freestanding

Site Plan of the Asilo

There are a number of salient reasons for the location of the building on the given site. Initially, we can tell by Terragni's early sketches that the square, like the *Casa del Fascio*, was going to be the primary form of the plan. Given that condition, Terragni rotated the plan to allow for the largest square that would be possible on the site. This move essentially created four complex shapes on all four sides of the building. By placing a regular shape onto the irregular site, Terragni guarantees that the 'value of absolute' geometric beauty would be imprinted onto the project.

This rotation was significant in numerous ways. It sets the building off from the traditional grid of the neighborhood, thereby identifying it as a building of special importance and an example of the new Fascist architecture. The rotation also brought the building closer to the cardinal axis, thereby aligning it with a larger order. Most importantly, the rotation forced the *Asilo* to face and focus on *Castel Baradello* in the distance. This rotational phenomenon is felt most strongly as a child ascends the stair/ramp to the playground on the roof. As each child would ascend this stair/ramp, they would be reminded of the government and its subsequent control. The *Baradello* tower became the school's de facto 'Lictor Tower', much in the same way that the Medieval *Torre Dei Conti* in Rome served a similar purpose for the *Danteum*.

The rotation resulted in the four aforementioned discreet spaces around the building. The north space became a garden/play area. The east space became an extension of the classrooms. The west space was utilized as an entrance to the basement and kitchen area. And the south space became the official entrance to the *Asilo* and was characterized by a subtle triangle that bore a marked resemblance to a similar space in front of the church in Como that Terragni frequented, namely *Sant Abbondio*.

This initial architectural move exhibited the depth with which Terragni was to execute many of the decisions that separated this building from his other projects.

Image 10: View showing the alignment of the roof stair with the Baradello Tower in the distance

Image 11: Site plan of the Asilo, showing the alignment of the Asilo with the Baradello Tower

The Plan

Terragni illustrated his principles in all aspects of his architecture, however, the plan seems to be paramount in his designs. The *Asilo*, in this sense, is no exception. As mentioned before, the rotated square with a central courtyard essentially describes the layout. The four classrooms are located on the east side of the building. They are the same size, and like the overall building, they rely on the square for their shape.

Located just to the south of the classrooms on the same side is the children's dressing room. This room is connected to the entry foyer and also to the hallway that separates it from the block of classrooms. The large playroom occupies the center of the plan and is aligned with the exterior courtyard. The foyer is located on the southeast corner of the playroom. This foyer is composed of glass on three sides, allowing parents who dropped off their children the opportunity to observe the playroom. The southern edge of the playroom is a large glass wall that negotiates between the building and the street. A linear balcony that extends the width of the playroom further articulates this edge. Photos suggest this balcony allowed a place for the children to wait for their parents.

Located on the west side of the playroom, in an alignment with the dressing room, is the administration. It consists of the director's office and an infirmary.

The refectory and the kitchen annex, protruding out of the effective square of the plan, dominates the west side of the building. The northern edge of the refectory houses the children's restrooms and an antechamber that was used for bathing.
The northern edge of the *Asilo* took the form of an open arcade that connected the bathroom wing with the classroom wing and

enclosed the courtyard on that side. The rooms of the *Asilo* are remarkable in that they all contain aspects of classical geometry and can be articulated as a complete form, yet they all have an aspect of transparency and flexibility that allows them to be understood in a number of ways.

Image 13: The balcony on the front of the Asilo >

Image 12: View of the playroom, showing the transparency out to the balcony and the street

Image 14: View of the doors in the playroom that lead to the director's office and the infirmary

The Structure

At first glance the structure of the *Asilo* seems fairly straightforward. Upon further examination, certain nuances reveal themselves. The structure is essentially a reinforced concrete frame that consists of seven bays in the east-west axis and five bays in the north-south axis. This system dictates that the bays are rectangular and not square. The columns themselves take a number of manifestations. The most common of these expressions is the simple rectangular column. These columns have an approximately 2:1 ratio in plan and are coinciding with the grid. Depending on their location, they are situated either in a north-south or an east-west direction.

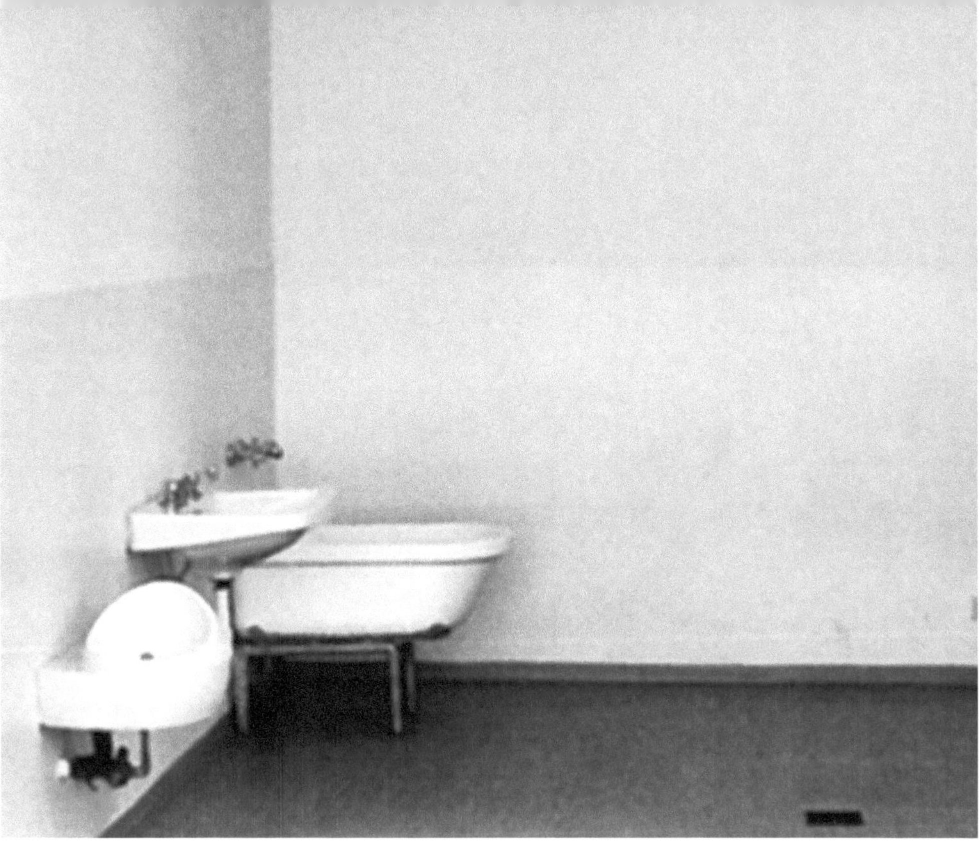

Image 15: View of the bathing area on the north edge of the refectory

Image 16: View of the exterior northern arcade (permission of Trevor Platt)

The orientation of the columns depended on the activity or direction of the room. For example, the columns in the playroom are all aligned north-south, towards the large glass openings that face the street and conversely the courtyard. In the classrooms, the columns face east-west, with the direction indicating the all-glass wall that faces the exterior classroom area. It is as if Terragni devised a system whereby the columns indicate either a direction of movement or view (north/south columns) or a static condition reflecting the functions of the rooms (east/west columns), as in the classrooms and the refectory.

The third type of structural support took the shape of a double column, which could then be described as a simple square. This hybrid condition appears primarily along the structural line of the east/west third row of columns. This might be due to an expansion joint of

Image 17: View of the columns in the refectory

some kind or to mark the transition between the different functional aspects of the school. The beams are mostly hidden with a plaster finish, which allows the columns to clarify the structural intentions.

Materials

The material palette of the *Asilo* is relatively simple. As mentioned, the building is a straightforward reinforced concrete structure. The resulting concrete columns are faced in plaster. The ceiling is also plastered, as are both the interior and exterior walls. All the plasterwork is rendered white, allowing the building to express its modernist roots. This material choice causes the building to stand out amongst its mostly gray stone or stucco neighbors.

Besides the plaster, glass makes up the majority of the rest of the material palette. There are, however, a number of critical excep-

Image 18: Exterior view of the Asilo illustrating the contrast between the building and its context

Image 19: The signage of the Asilo

tions. The front of the *Asilo* has a thin stone base that marks it as a building that is not merely functional and relates it to an Italian tradition. Also, the signage of the *Asilo* is rendered in a series of stone plaques, each representing one letter of the name. The sign appears to be of a similar stone to that used in the base, however, it has a more refined finish.

The exterior floors are all rendered in a flagstone that is typical of the region. The interior floors are all covered in gray linoleum. The window and doorframes are painted metal with stone sills. Terragni has utilized a minimal amount of materials to allow for the space and geometry to be recognized and appreciated. The small section of glass block floor in the director's office allows light to penetrate down to the basement, serving as the sole distinction in terms of materiality.

Plan Relationship to the Roman Plan of Como

The plan of the *Asilo* is not a standard plan on a number of levels. At first glance, the plan appears to be a typical classical-modern plan. Closer inspection of the plan reveals a sensibility that is both critical and historical. Initial analysis of the plan exposes a series of non-alignments of the axes. These non-alignments tend to extend from, and be a result of, the shifts in the plan.

Where did these shifts come from? Examining the ancient Roman plan of Como gives us hints as to the possible origin of these non-alignments. The Roman plan of Como differs from many of the typical Roman plans of Italian cities in that the *Cardo* and *Decumanus* do not extend directly through the city, but instead are forced to shift to minor roads that then terminate at the city gates. It is worth noting that Terragni manipulated the circulation paths of the *Asilo* so that the alignments are not entirely lineal, but were instead slightly shifted to perhaps make one more aware of their location and simultaneously make the project more contextual to the city of Como.

If we break down the circulation axes in the *Asilo* into two different types, that of 'major' and 'shifted', we can further examine these phenomena. First, we can identify three separate 'major' circulation axes, two that are aligned in the north-south direction and one that

Image 20: The plan of the Asilo, showing the slight shifts in axis of the various paths

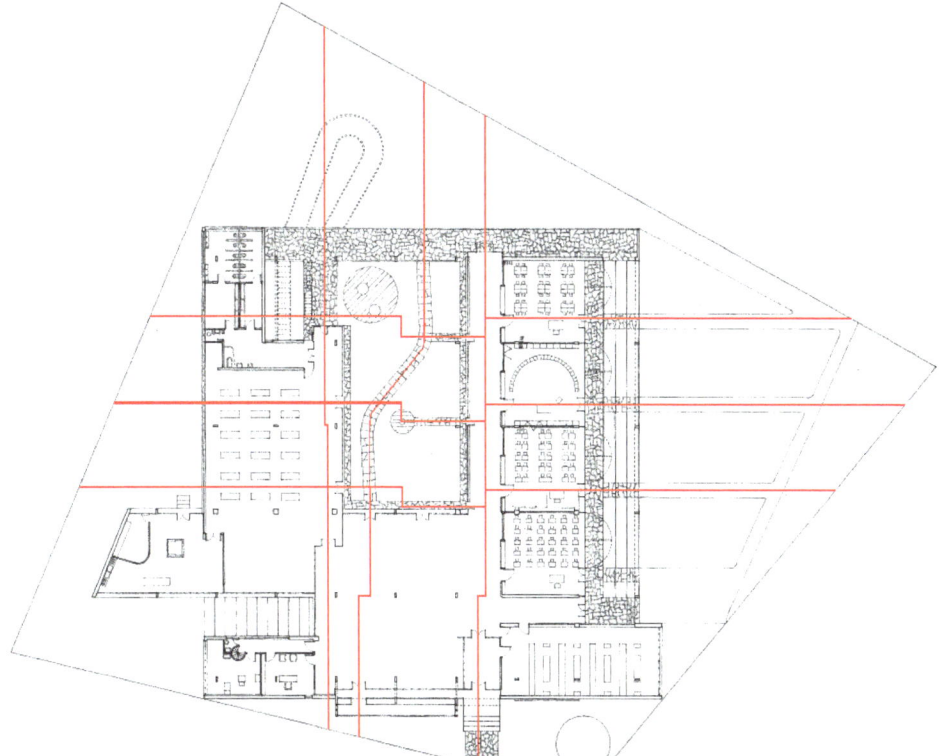

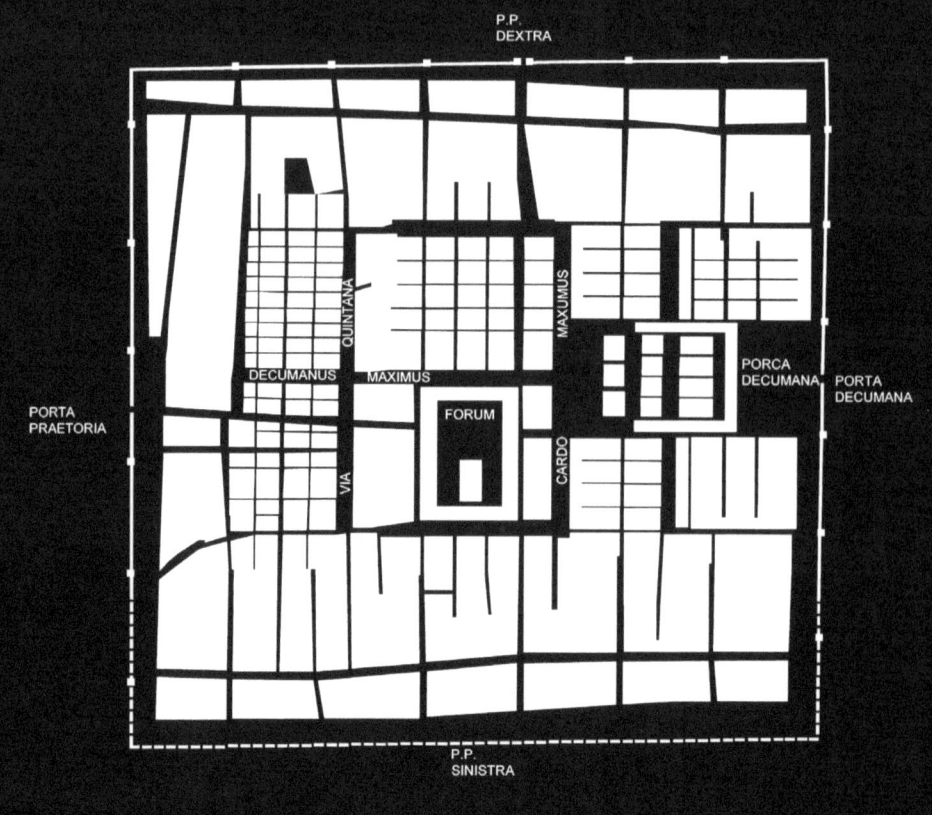

Image 21: The Roman plan of Como, illustrating the shifts of various axes in the city

is aligned in the east-west direction. The first of these axes occurs along the east side of the courtyard, beginning at the entrance and running past the side of the playroom. It continues past the four classrooms and finally culminates in the doors that lead out to the garden. The second axis is perpendicular to this fist axis and begins

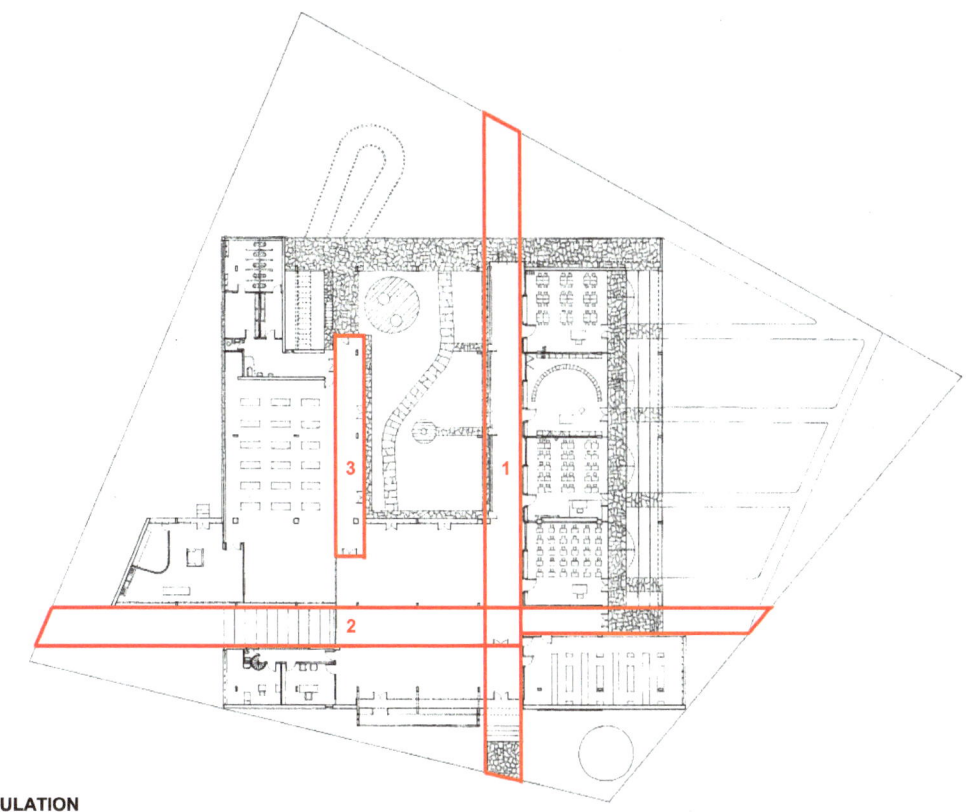

Image 22: Plan of the Asilo, illustrating the three major circulation axes

at the door between the changing room and the first classroom on the east side. It then extends across the middle of the playroom and culminates in the large glass window that overlooks the subterranean entrance to the basement. The third and final 'major' axis starts at the door between the playroom and the refectory and extends along the west side, culminating in the door that leads out to the garden.

The north-south axes shift slightly. The doors that begin the axes do not align with the doors that end the axes. In other words, if one follows the axis from the front entry door, it continues through the foyer unaffected and then is forced to shift slightly to the right in order to end on the exit door at the end of the hallway. The other north-south axis that extends through the refectory is also forced to shift slightly to the right in order to exit through the door into the garden. A third minor north-south axis begins at the glass doors that lead to the balcony on the south side; this axis is forced to shift to the right in order to accommodate the door on the other side of the playroom that leads to the path through the courtyard.

This path is then literally shifted, in a curvilinear fashion, as it extends through the courtyard toward the garden. There are also three shifting paths that extend from the east side to the west. These three axes all begin at the glass doors of the three northern-most classrooms that connect the classrooms to their respective exterior spaces. The axes continue across the classroom and then shift to the left in the corridor to accommodate the glass doors that lead out into the courtyard. The two southern most axes ultimately shift back and align with the doors on the west side of the courtyard.

What is remarkable about these shifting axes is the realization that it would have been very easy for Terragni to align everything, achieving a balanced and predictable outcome. Instead, these slight shifts yield a richer reading of the shifting-rectangles phenomenon, an anti-classical idea, and possibly a reference to the ancient plan of Como.

Proportions
The proportions of the *Asilo* plan depend on the three forms deployed throughout. Terragni has orchestrated an ingenious diagram whereby squares, diagons, and the golden section all overlap and simultaneously exist, ultimately producing a plan that allows a multivalent reading.

Squares
The entire structure is based on the square, as it is the primary geometry of the plan. The plan, in its entirety, describes the first square. This initial square extends slightly beyond the east elevation of the classrooms, but is aligned with the edge of the exterior of the

Image 23: View of the courtyard showing the curved path through the courtyard

dressing room that extends out. This line is actually marked by a line of stones on the ground. The four classrooms that occupy the east side of the building are all squares in plan. These classrooms, like the overall plan, identify this primary shape as a critical component of the building's geometry.

The third square of the *Asilo* occupies the playroom, and is formed by the inclusion of the two front structural bays with the exterior balcony. Terragni was able to show both a shift in the plan as well as the strategy of transparency with this spatial move.

A fourth square is formed by slightly increasing the third square until is it extends to the far east wall of the playroom and to the edge of the foyer and upward until it coincides with the entry wall of the refectory.

Image 24: Plan diagrams showing the various squares inscribed in the Asilo

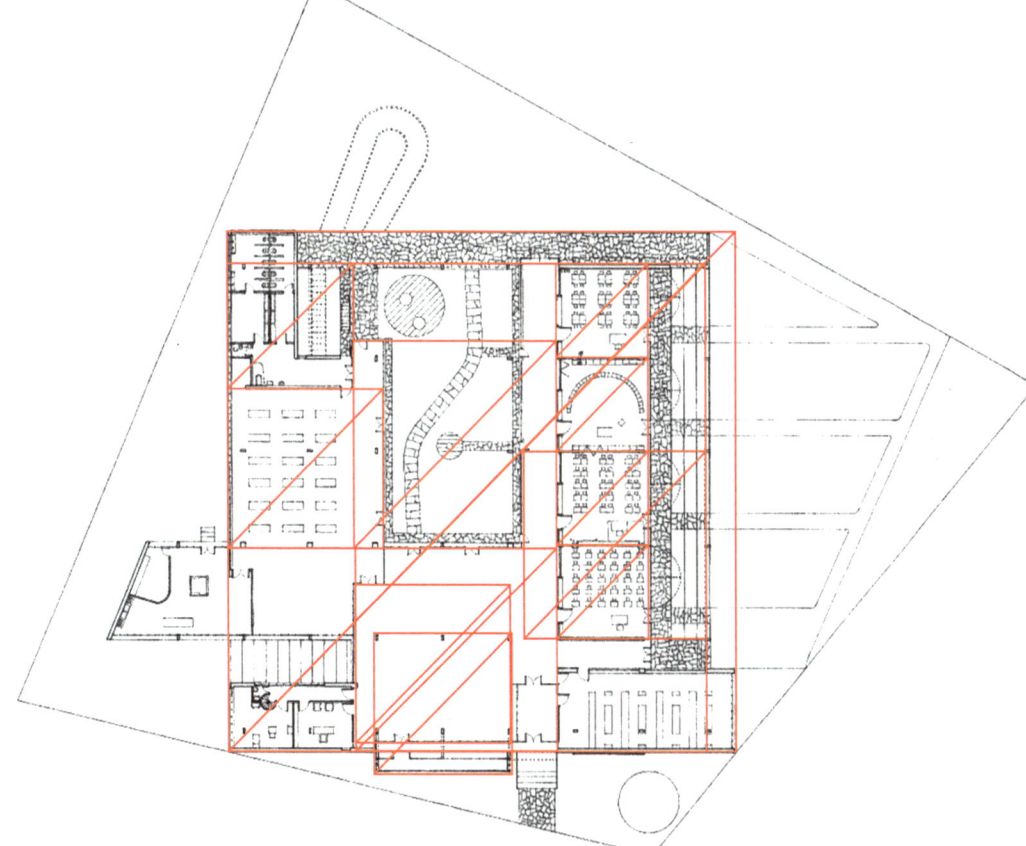

Image 25: Plan of the Asilo with all the squares illustrated in composite

The fifth square is again based on the playroom, however here Terragni has included the entire room with the overlap of the foyer in one corner and conversely the overlap of the refectory in the opposite corner.

The sixth square is formed by the combination of three different functions. Terragni has combined the hallway with two classrooms and their respective exterior spaces to culminate in this square.

The seventh square, like the third, is centered, however this time on the exterior courtyard. The square is completed by the inclusion of the main hallway and the corresponding space in the refectory.

The eighth square is inscribed in the overall space of the refectory, which exists between the glass wall of the courtyard and the west wall in one direction and the back wall of the refectory and the larger columns that indicate a mid-point of the overall plan.

The ninth square in located primarily on the service zone in the northwest corner of the building. It includes the two stairs to the roof, the cleaning room, the janitor's closet, and most of the restrooms.

There is a tenth square that is dictated more by the exterior columns on the east and north sides. This square is very similar to the overall square, but slightly smaller as a way of recognizing the planes of the vertical structural elements.

Golden Ratio

The golden ratio of the *Asilo* is the most dominant of the geometries at play in the plan of the building. There are numerous golden rectangles inscribed into the plan. They can be examined in terms of the ones that are vertically oriented and those that are conversely oriented in the horizontal. Beyond this, Terragni used the golden rectangle as a way of grouping spaces and more importantly, as a way of constructing space.

Vertical

The first vertical golden ratio occurs in the central courtyard and forms the center of the scheme. It is worth noting that the path that crosses the courtyard forms an angle that is identical to the diagonal of the golden ratio. Like the squares of the classrooms, this sets a standard of geometric design and concept that is seen throughout the design decisions of the building.

The second vertical golden ratio essentially delineates the group of the northern most three classrooms, including their respective exterior spaces as wells as the adjoining hallway.

A third vertical golden ratio occurs primarily in the refectory to the west of the courtyard. The golden ratio begins along the same line as the previous two (this line seems to represent a structural line in that the columns are doubled along this line, indicating an important threshold) and subsequently extends to the entire width of the refectory, culminating in the wall of the toilet room. Terragni has used this geometry as a way of organizing the three main spaces in the northern half of the plan.

The fourth vertical golden ratio is found primarily in the playroom and is formed by extending a golden ratio from the outer most edge of the exterior balcony through the room and ending at the glass wall of the courtyard. This forms a golden ratio that employs walls and rails as its border in one direction, but depends on the structural columns as its other.

There are consequently two more vertical golden sections formed by the combination of two of the classrooms on the eastern edge. Notice that the stone walkway on the exterior is included in these. The bathrooms in the northwest corner of the building inscribe a sixth vertical golden section.

A seventh vertical golden section can be seen in the exterior stair that is adjacent to the bathrooms.

There is an eighth vertical golden section that occupies the small foyer that opens to the bathing room next to the bathrooms and to the north garden.

Finally there is a ninth vertical section that occupies the glass foyer in the southeast corner of the playroom.

Horizontal
The first horizontal golden ratio occupies the entire northern half of the *Asilo*. It originates at the structural line that effectively delin-

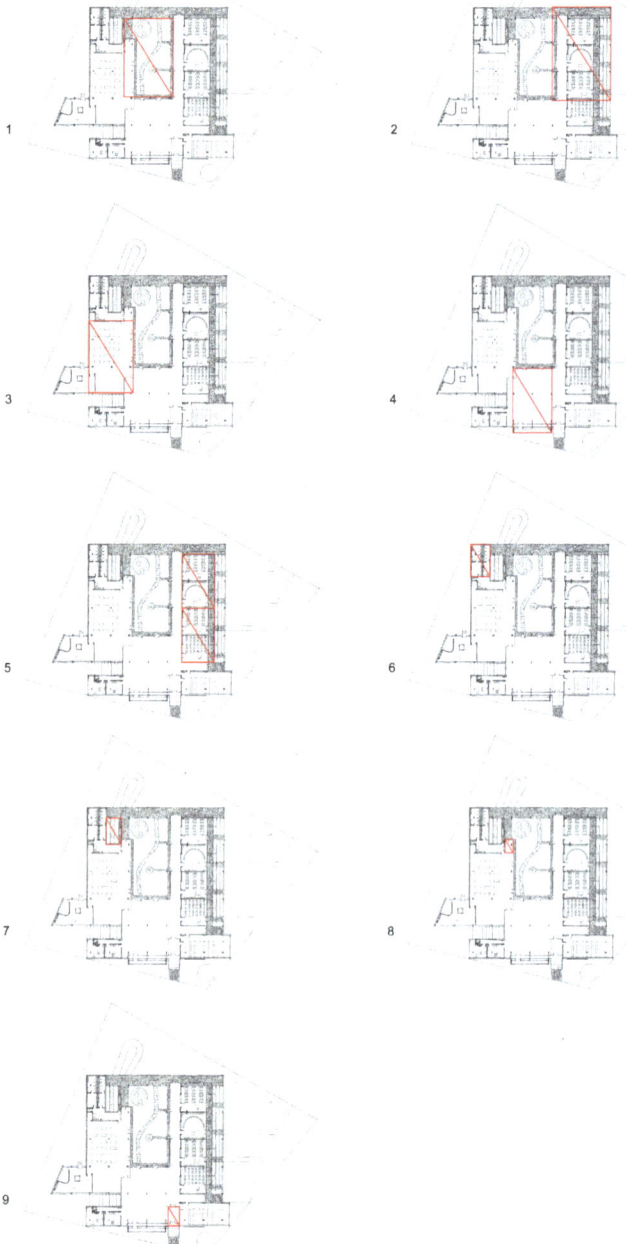

Image 26: Plan diagrams showing the various vertical golden sections

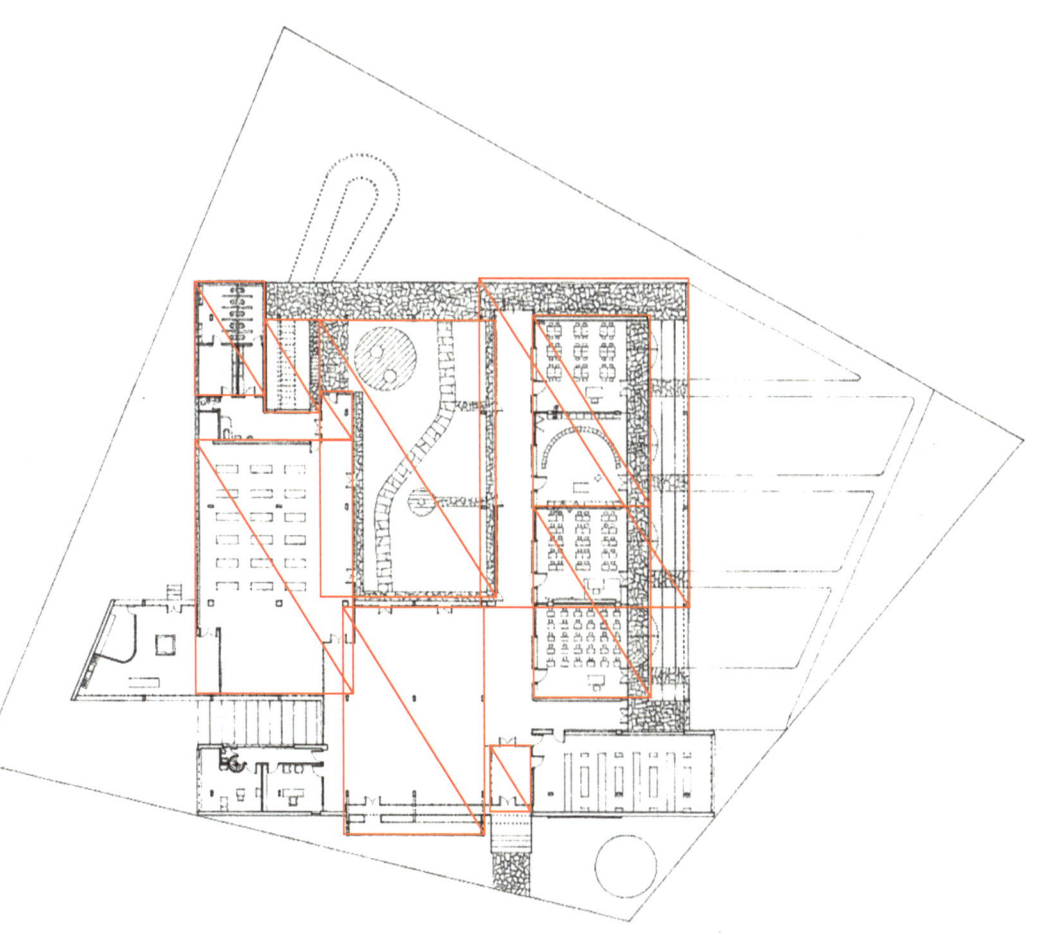

Image 27: Plan of the Asilo with all the vertical golden sections in composite

eates the edge of the courtyard and extends to the northern edges of the building in the north direction. It ultimately encompasses the refectory with its service functions, the courtyard, and three of the classrooms.

The second, horizontal golden ratio takes the form of the individual classrooms with their respective exterior space included. This condition is rational in that the classrooms have already established the square as their primary shape, and by the addition of the exterior teaching space they form a golden ratio.

The third horizontal golden ratio occupies the northern portion of the playroom. It essentially begins at the north edge of the foyer and extends to fill the rest of the playroom including the entrance to the refectory.

The fourth horizontal golden rectangle occupies the dressing room and the adjacent hallway. One can see how Terragni utilized geometry as a way of dictating the sizes of various spaces and paths.

The fifth and sixth horizontal golden ratios are the same size and overlap. Coincidentally, they are also the same size as the second horizontal golden ratio that dictates the classroom. The fifth one occupies the space at the southern end of the refectory, overlapping with the playroom on one side and the kitchen on the other. The sixth essentially occupies the kitchen, overlapping with the refectory. The seventh horizontal golden ratio describes the combination of the service ramp and the administrative hallway.

Diagons
The diagon is a shape that has fascinated architects and artists for centuries. A diagon is formed by simply inscribing a diagonal across a square, then rotating that diagonal down until it coincides with the edge of the square. This simple act forms the diagon. What is interesting about the diagon is that when you add two diagons together, you create a third. This is the only shape that has this particular quality. This reference to the whole has placed the diagon into a position that differs from all other geometries. In the *Asilo*, Terragni utilized the diagon primarily as a way of organizing the structural grid of the building.

Shifting Rectangles
The plans of Terragni's projects often can be categorized as a series of shifting rectangles. This phenomenon is illustrated in the *Asilo* perhaps more than any other of his projects. The plan of the *Asilo*

is comprised of four basic rectangles. These rectangles describe the classroom wing, the playroom, the refectory, and the courtyard, setting up a language and system that permeates the building and allows for a multitude of readings.

There are constant overlaps that occur between these spaces, encouraging a breakdown not only between the inside and outside, but also between various rooms or areas. This occurs throughout the building but is perhaps most noticeable when occupying the spaces adjacent to the courtyard. It is easy to observe the implications of this spatial overlap and layering. When visitors are walking along the edge of the refectory, it is clearly implied that they are also in the courtyard. This can also be experienced whilst on the balcony near the entrance. Here one is both on the balcony, but also still part of the playroom. Ultimately there are numerous instances in the building that allow this double reading.

Relationship to Radice

The painter Mario Radice was a close friend of Terragni's and is certainly an inspiration to his spatially and graphically intricate constructions. Radice's work of the 1930s was particularly influential to Terragni. Radice was executing paintings that explored this abstract relationship between rectangular planes. The result was both a straightforward graphic interest, but also a phenomenal spatial implication. Paintings such as *Composizione 2*, *Composizione 22*, and *Composizione C.F.* all point to a concrete relationship with architecture.

It is poignant that Terragni was able to synthesize these ideas into a true spatial form of architecture rather than a mere pictorial representation. Terragni was never slavish in his adoption of Radice's principles, but he was extremely inventive in how he could incorporate these motifs into his work on multiple levels.

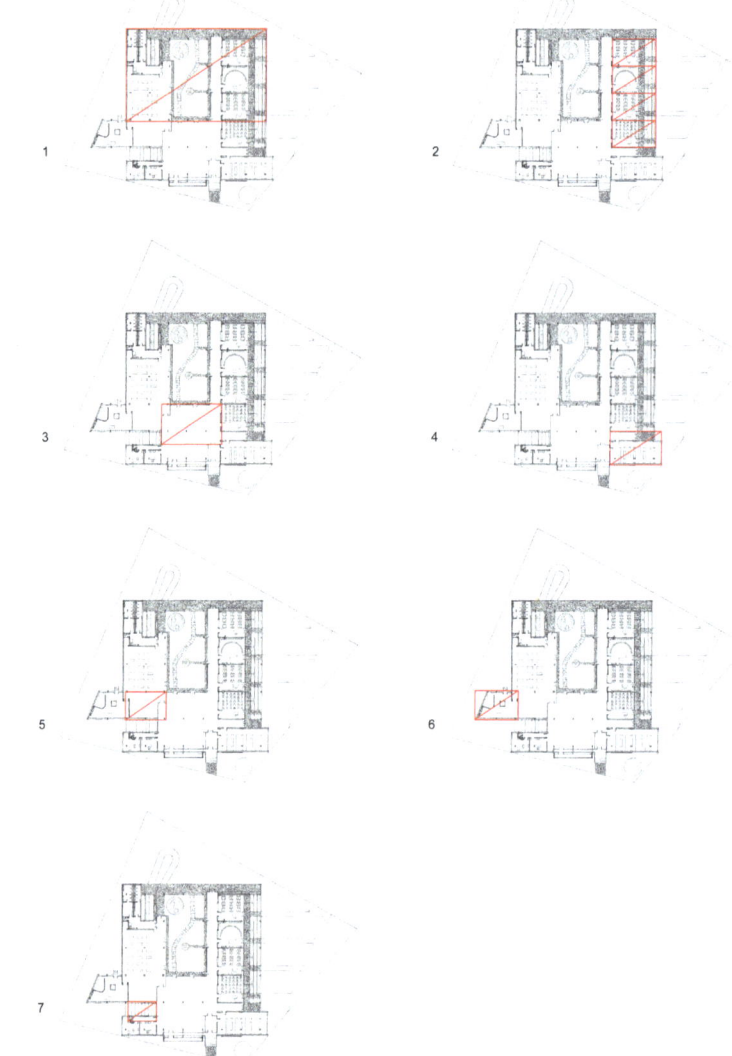

Image 28: Plan diagrams showing the various horizontal golden sections

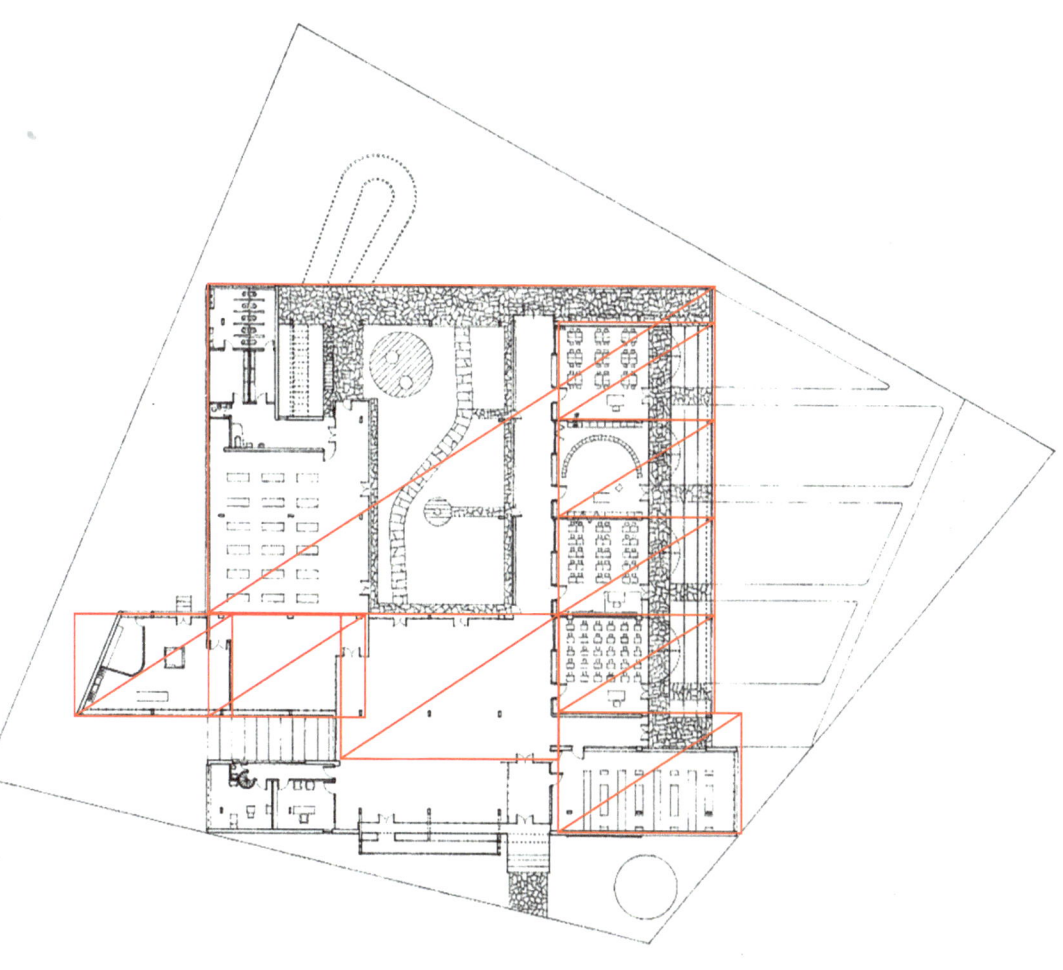

Image 29: Plan of the Asilo with all the horizontal golden sections in composite

One need only view the fresco by Radice that ornamented the main conference room in the *Casa del Fascio* in Como to observe this phenomenon. In that composition, there are numerous possible Terragni projects. A number of Terragni's other projects shared

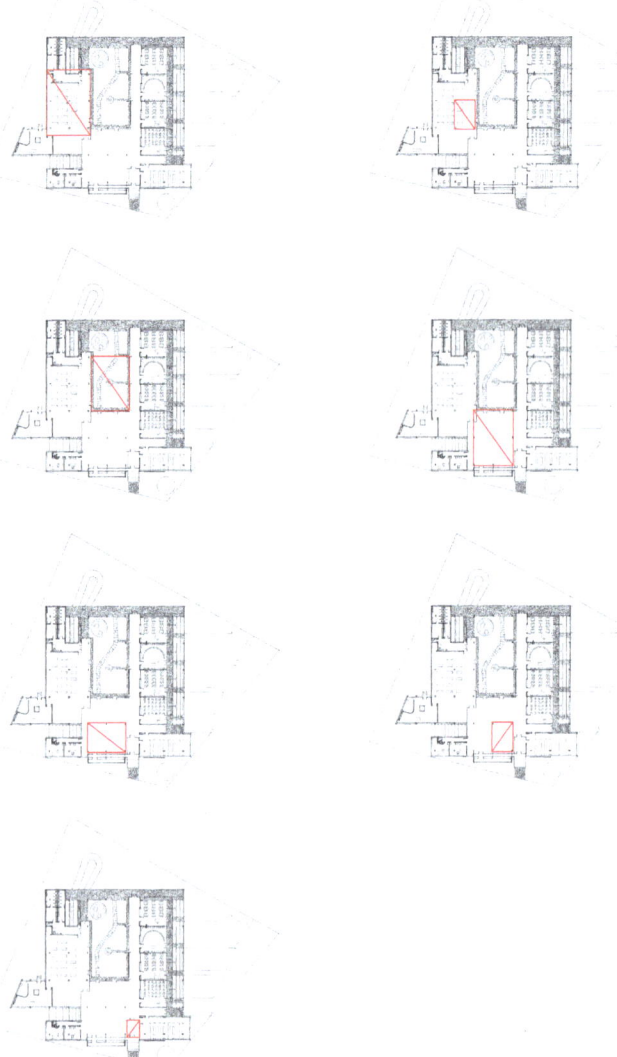

Image 30: Plan diagrams showing the various diagons

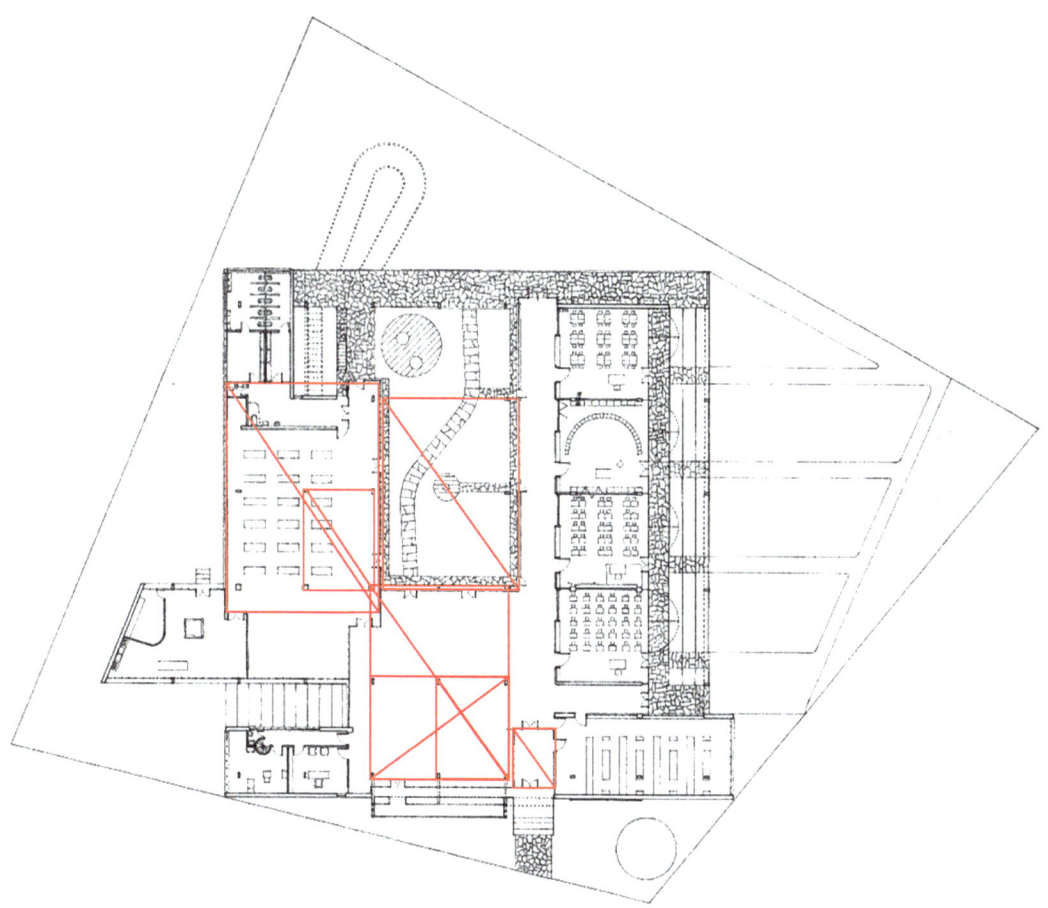

Image 31: Plan of the Asilo with all the diagons in composite

this shifting rectangle language, most clearly Terragni's *Casa Floricoltare*, the *Villa Bianca,* and the library competition in Lugano that he executed with Lingeri.

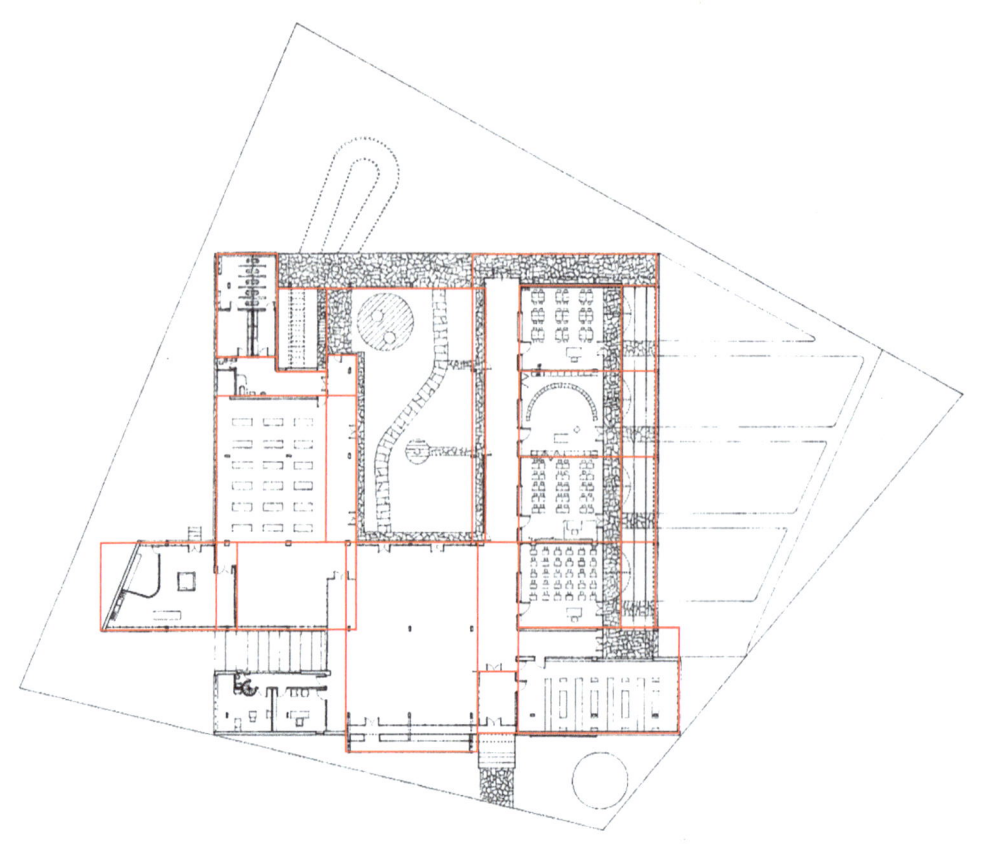

Image 32: Plan of the Asilo showing shifting rectangles

Flexibility

The *Asilo* employed a series of flexible architectural devices. The most visible of these elements are the sun-shading fixtures that are located along the east side of the building, adjacent to the classrooms. A motorized assembly that allowed the occupants to control the amount of sunlight during the morning hours operated all these shading screens. It operated at the scale of the classrooms as well as the adjoining exterior spaces. Cattaneo employed a very similar element at the *Casa d'affitto* in Cernobbio.

Terragni also utilized a series of canvas sun-shading devices on the balcony on the entry façade. The glass walls of the classrooms were also flexible in that they could be opened entirely, thereby erasing

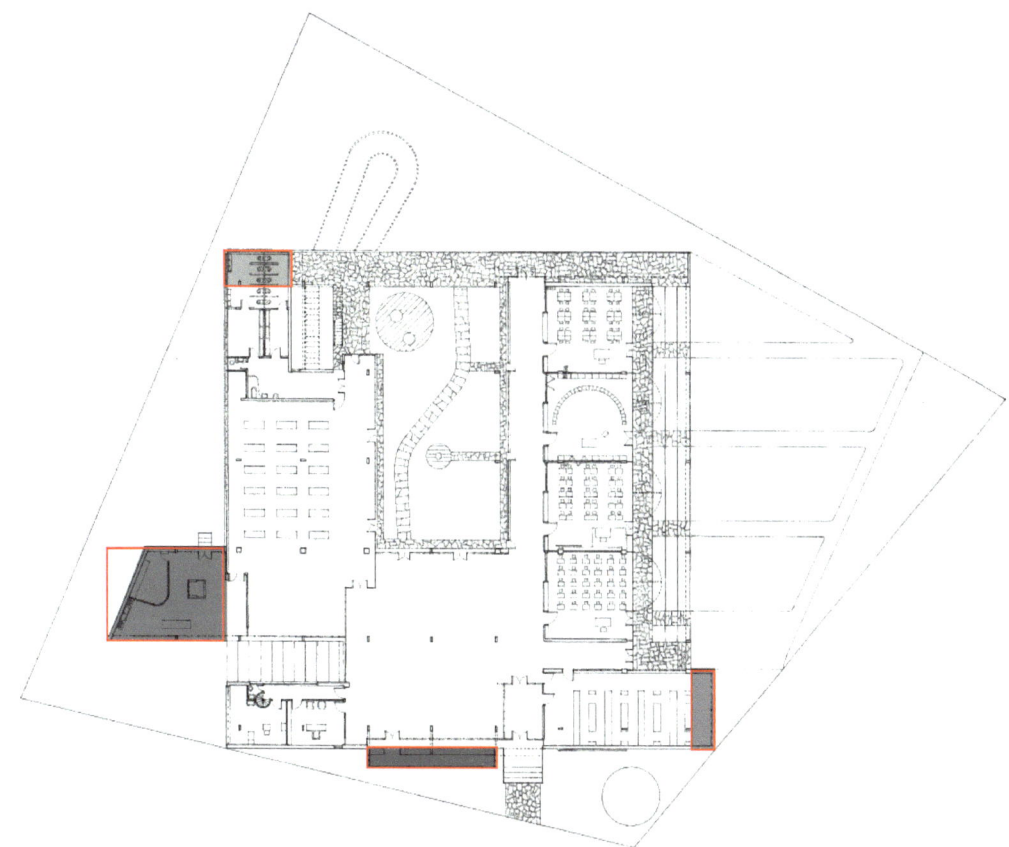

Image 33: Plan of the Asilo showing the "end zones"

Image 34: The glass wall of the refectory allowing spatial extension to the courtyard

the barrier between the interior and exterior. Unfortunately, the radiators were also placed along this glass wall (meaning the breakdown was merely visual) and the students could not flow out to the exterior learning space.

The flexibility continued in the classrooms, taking the form of the walls that separated them. There are four classrooms in the *Asilo,* and consequently, three walls separating them. These walls were moveable and could fold away allowing the classrooms to spatially join together or ultimately transform into one very large

Image 35: The front porch as an extension of the playroom >

room. The first classroom had a series of kinetic metal frames that occupied the southern wall. One of the frames was a black chalkboard; the other was a frame that contained a photograph of Mussolini. These two frames were connected by a series of wires and weights. As one frame moved, the other followed suit. Here, Terrragni has captured the concept of the project, 'shifting rectangles', and has transformed it into a piece of flexible furniture.

Elevations and Sections

The East and South elevations of the *Asilo* are very well considered and the discussion will be primarily concerned with these two. Let us first reflect on the South elevation, which is also considered the primary façade that functions as the entry. This façade is primarily a simple flat plaster wall, marked only by a stone base and a small coping at the top. There is a large opening in the wall. This opening, which is not quite centered, is actually part of the large balcony that dominates the elevation. The glass wall is recessed, allowing the balcony to float away from the building.

The balcony structure, which extends from three separate columns in the playroom, is articulated in such a way that it resembles a

Image 36: The operable sunshade devices on the east side

building within a building. It is also justified to the left, allowing the entrance to occur on the right. There are two more operations that take place on this elevation. One is the vertical window on the left side of the balcony, the other is the horizontal signage that exists on the right side of the entrance.

This dichotomy of vertical versus horizontal reading is common and occurs throughout the building. Beyond this basic description, there is also a series of relationships that mark this elevation as a significant part of the project (see Image 40 on page 108). If one looks at the glass elevation of the kitchen, beyond what might be considered the actual elevation, it is a measurement denoted by the letter 'Z'. This measurement is also the distance between the edge of the elevation proper and the right side of the director's vertical window. Again, if one measures the distance between the edge of the left side of the elevation proper to the edge of the balcony opening, it can be denoted by the letter 'Y'. This measurement equals the length of the balcony structure. Finally, the large glass opening, which shall be labeled 'X', is subsequently equal to the right side of the elevation. Terragni has devised a system that relies on its various parts to construct the whole. This relation of part to whole is fundamental to Terragni's architecture and this elevation provides a paramount example.

The other elevation that shall be discussed is the East elevation, primarily comprised of the four classrooms. This elevation is remarkably simple and is merely a reflection of the functions. The dressing room is rendered as a straightforward glass wall, with a stone base that extends from the South elevation. To the right of this window wall are the doors that allow entrance into the hallway. This set of doors is essentially identical to the windows of the dressing room, except for the operable factor. The classrooms, which occupy the remainder of the elevation, are four identical glass walls that are comprised of a system that allows for the complete opening of

Image 37: View of shifting metal frames (chalkboard) in the classroom

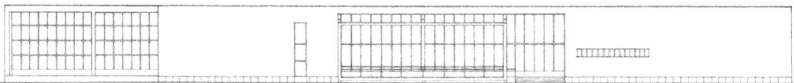
Image 38: South elevation of the Asilo

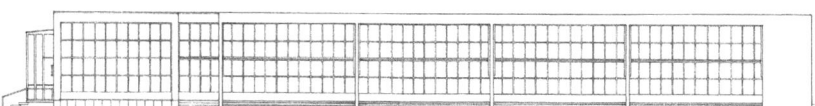
Image 39: East elevation of the Asilo

the classrooms, encouraging a complete breakdown of the barrier between the interior and exterior. Each classroom also has a single glass door allowing access to the exterior classrooms. Located in front of these glass walls is an arcade of columns that designates the spatial limits of the exterior classroom and also supports the operable sun shading devices on that elevation. It is interesting that this arcade, while being the most recognizable part of the structure, in reality has very little true structure and is instead a frame used as an abstract ordering device. This frame is also the culmination of the reading of going from 'dense' to 'frame' to 'open'.

In terms of proportions, this elevation utilizes the golden ratio as its medium. Each pane of glass in the elevation is proportionally a golden ratio. The overall window wall of the dressing room is a golden ratio, the glass wall of the hallway entry door is a vertical golden ratio, and finally, each of the four openings in the arcade describes a golden ratio. Again, Terragni has skillfully negotiated this compositional problem and has produced an elevation that is both clear and concise, but also contains a precise proportional system that governs it on a compositional level.

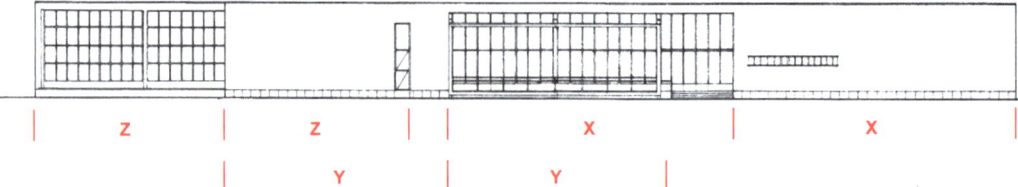

Image 40: Diagram showing the proportional relationships of the South elevation of the Asilo

The elevations can be discussed on some other levels as well, most particularly their relationship to transparency and the balance of vertical and horizontal. Transparency is prominent in most of the building, however the East elevation of the classrooms and the South elevation at the entrance certainly bear further mention. The entry façade is remarkable on many levels, but its transparency is truly singular. Here, Terragni has constructed the glass house of education. Anyone on the street can walk past the *Asilo* and clearly see into the building and can observe the children and the teachers at work.

This transparency was crucial to the Italian Fascist philosophy, convincing the masses that their government was indeed a government with nothing to hide. This façade speaks to the fact that the Italians thought of Fascism as beneficial to the people. The reflections and refractions there also provide a sense of movement or vibration. This implication of movement or dynamism imbues the building, and thereby the government, with the same quality.

The balcony that is so prominent on this elevation undoubtedly reinforced this perception. It served as a porch that allowed the children to wait for their parents to collect them. The other elevation that utilized transparency was the East, which represented the four classrooms. Like the South elevation, this one was completely glass and allowed a full view into each classroom. The passerby could view the children at play or while learning.

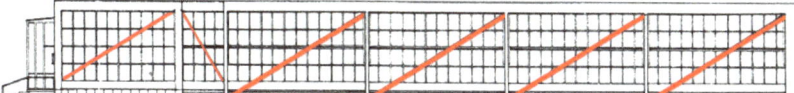

Image 41: Diagram showing golden section proportions on the East elevation of the Asilo

Beyond this, the glass wall encouraged the perception and the literal breakdown between the interior and exterior. The idea of fresh air and sunshine as an integral part of a child's education was incorporated into the design.

The last walls that truly utilized transparency were the East and North facing walls of the courtyard. The east-facing wall separates the courtyard from the refectory and is primarily visual in that there are only two smaller doors that allow students to enter and exit. The north-facing glass wall separates the courtyard from the playroom and also contains two doors, one that aligns with the before-mentioned curved path. The second door opens to the small lawn. This glass wall allows the spatial explosion of the playroom to continue completely through the building, from the entry street through to the garden at the back of the site.

Another area that celebrates transparency is the hallway adjacent to the four classrooms. When one is occupying this hallway, a view is allowed (at eye level) into each of the classrooms and conversely at the same level into the courtyard. The two windows are at the same height and mirror each other on either side of the hallway, allowing the transparency to extend into the classrooms and subsequently into the courtyard.

Terragni uses a relationship of the vertical and the horizontal as a constant reference throughout the building. This is perhaps most

Image 42: The glass house of education

evident at the main entry façade where the vertical window of the director's office is offset by the horizontality of the *Asilo* signage. The west-facing courtyard elevation is yet another example of this balancing act; here the horizontal windows are poised against the verticality of the freestanding columns and their adjacent vertical windows. This motive is used in numerous places within the building, setting up a balanced yet adversarial composition.

This constant battle of vertical and horizontal, as well as the transparency and dynamic quality of the elevations, reminds one of the elevations of the Capitoline Hill and the chancel of St. Peter's, both executed by Terragni's idol, Michelangelo.

Furniture and Fixtures

Terragni went beyond the design of the building and designed all aspects of the environment as well, specifically the furniture. He designed the desk for the director and re-utilized the design of the chairs that had previously been completed for the *Casa del Fascio*. Terragni also modified the *Casa del Fascio* chair to produce a children's version, without the arms. These small chairs compliment the overall design concept of the building.

Terragni worked with local craftsmen to produce multiple aspects of the *Asilo*, including the desks, chairs, windows, doors, and the remarkable spiral stair to the basement that is located adjacent to the director's office. Essentially, Terragni seems to have had a hand in everything except, perhaps, for the light fixtures which are in the form of simple white glass balls.

The colors used in the *Asilo* are also very telling in their restraint. Terragni used primarily gray and white, with the occasional red detail. As mentioned previously, the floors were gray linoleum throughout and the walls were rendered white. The steel fixtures of the doors and windows were also painted gray. The stalls in the bathroom, colored blue and pink, identify the gender of the separate sides of the room.

Image 43: Glass wall of the playroom showing the visual extension to the courtyard

Image 44: Horizontal windows in the hallway allowing views into the classrooms

Image 45: Vertical windows in the hallway showing the exterior columns (Vertical vs. Horizontal)

Image 46: Chair designed for the Asilo

9

Conclusion

Designing Without Adjectives

I was initially attracted to Guiseppe Terragni's *Asilo D'Infanzia Sant'Elia* for its timeless nature, stemming from a belief in absolutes. These absolutes form a concept that allows for a conviction that there is an appropriate response to any given problem. This is a modern concept that has systematically been swept aside in the wave of relativism that can be termed 'post-modern'. Terragni worked with a series of values or principles, and these tenets allowed him to produce an architecture that was outside the vagaries of fashion and was not subject to the adjectives of relativism.

This of course does not mean that one cannot describe a Terragni building as beautiful or exciting. The Fascist architect and critic Marcello Piacentini put forward the concept of "designing without adjectives." Piacentini believed in legitimate principles, as opposed to falling into the trap of describing one's work with self-serving adjectives that do not correspond to empirical facts. I believe that Terragni understood this implicitly and subsequently followed suit. As a professor I constantly reference this discipline to students. They are often uncomfortable with this concept and instead exercise their desire to attach descriptive terms to their work that they naively believe will sway others. Terragni's great lesson for students of architecture is that buildings are not political, adjectives are.

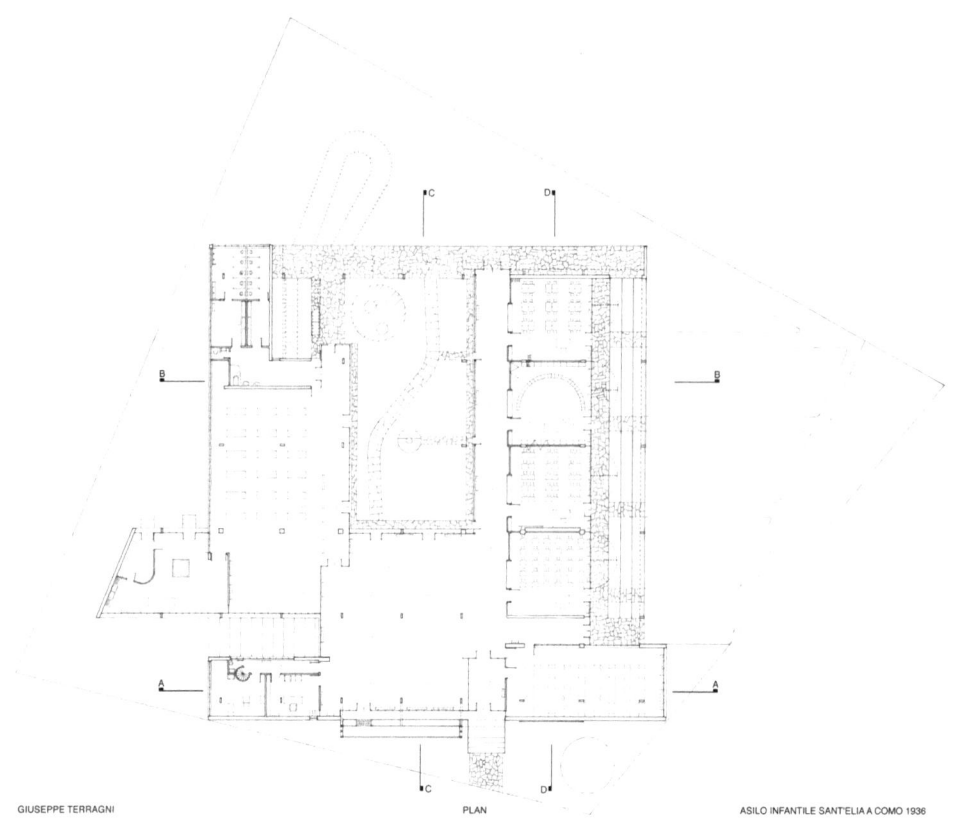

Image 1: Plan of the Asilo

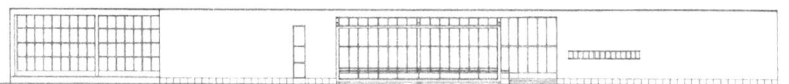

Image 2: South Elevation of the Asilo

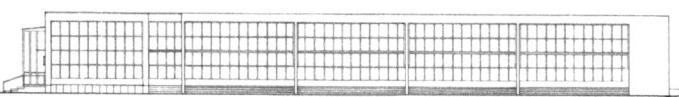

Image 3: East Elevation of the Asilo

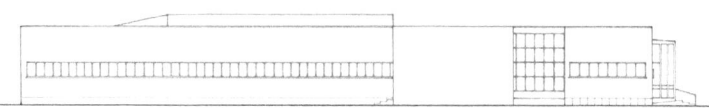

Image 4: West Elevation of the Asilo

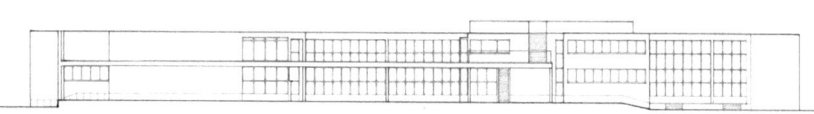

Image 5: North Elevation of the Asilo

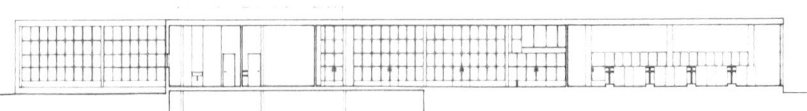

Image 6: Section through the offices, the playroom and the dressing rooms

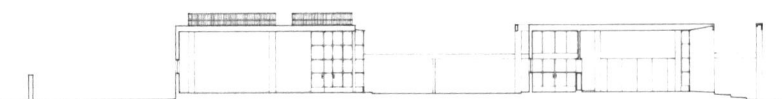

Image 7: Section through the refectory, the courtyard and the classrooms

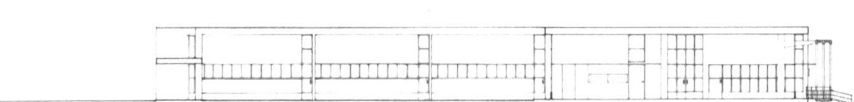

Image 8: Section through the courtyard and the playroom

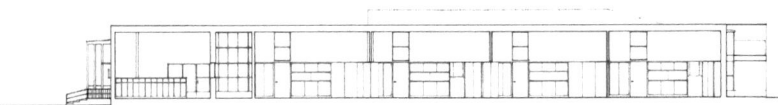

Image 9: Section through the dressing room and the classrooms

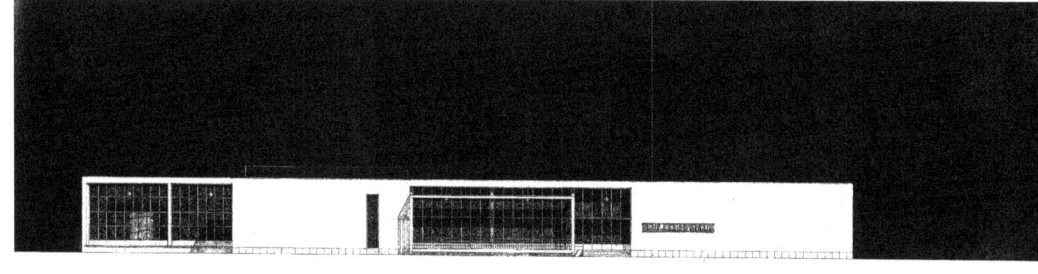

Image 10: Rendered South Elevation of the Asilo

Image 11: Rendered East Elevation of the Asilo

Image 12: Rendered West Elevation of the Asilo

Image 13: Rendered North Elevation of the Asilo

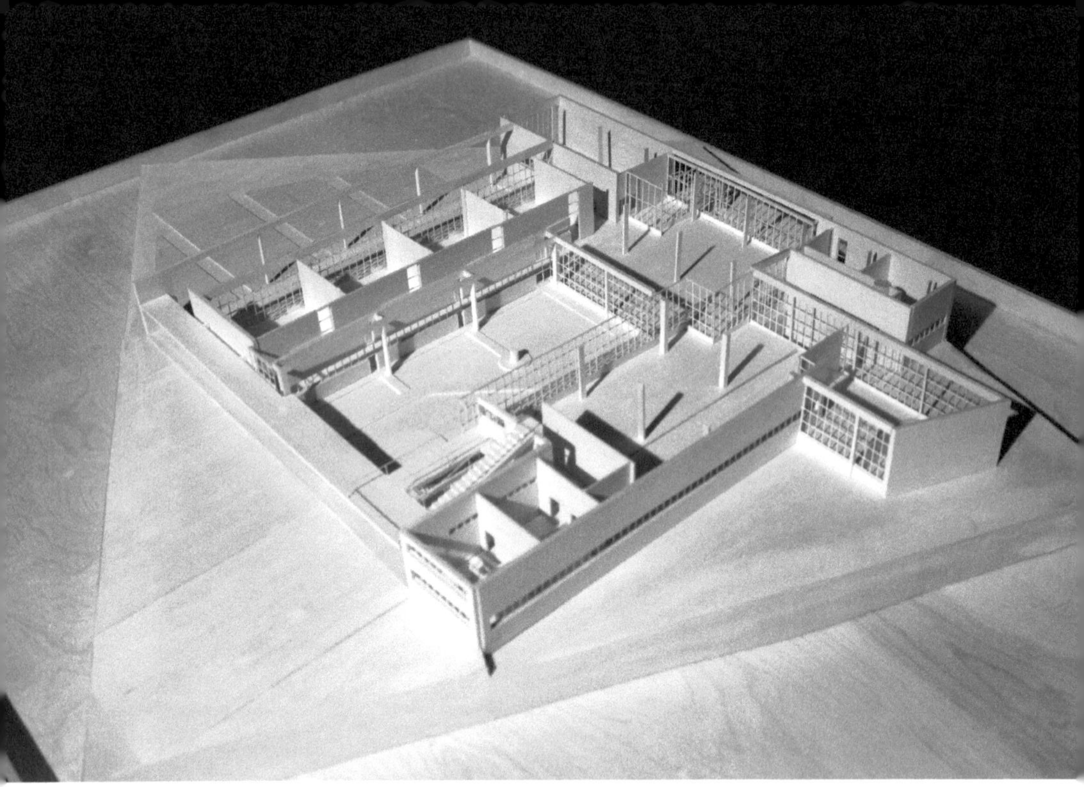

Image 14: Model of the Asilo from the Northwest

Image 15: Model of the Asilo from the Northeast

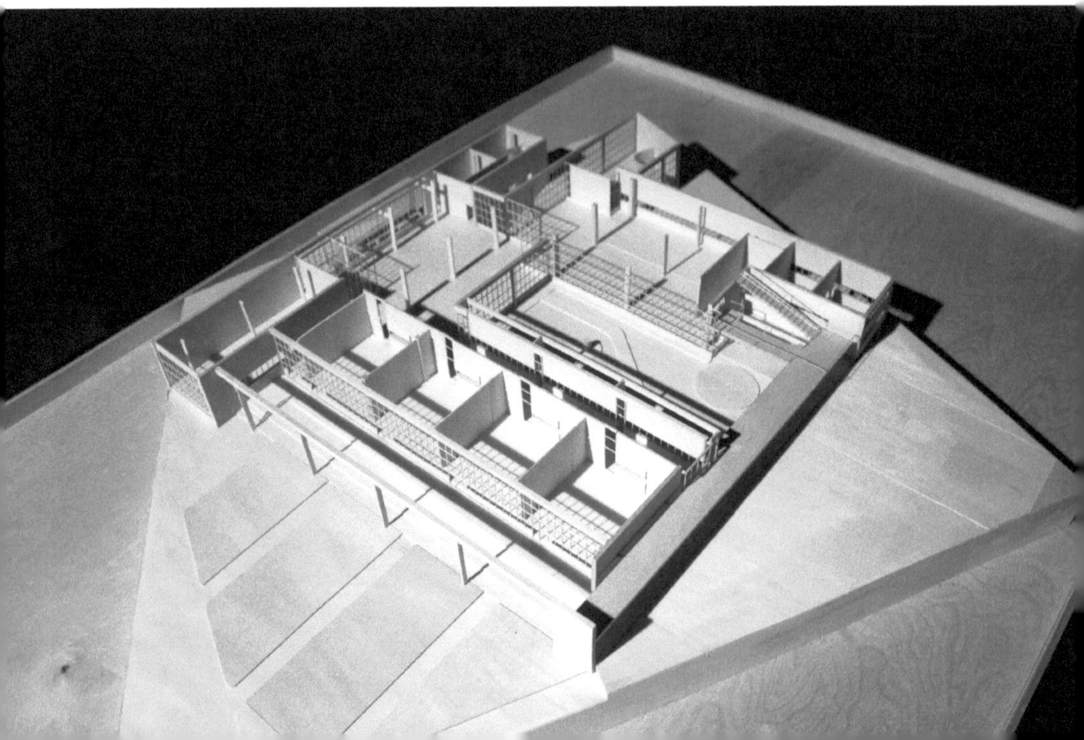

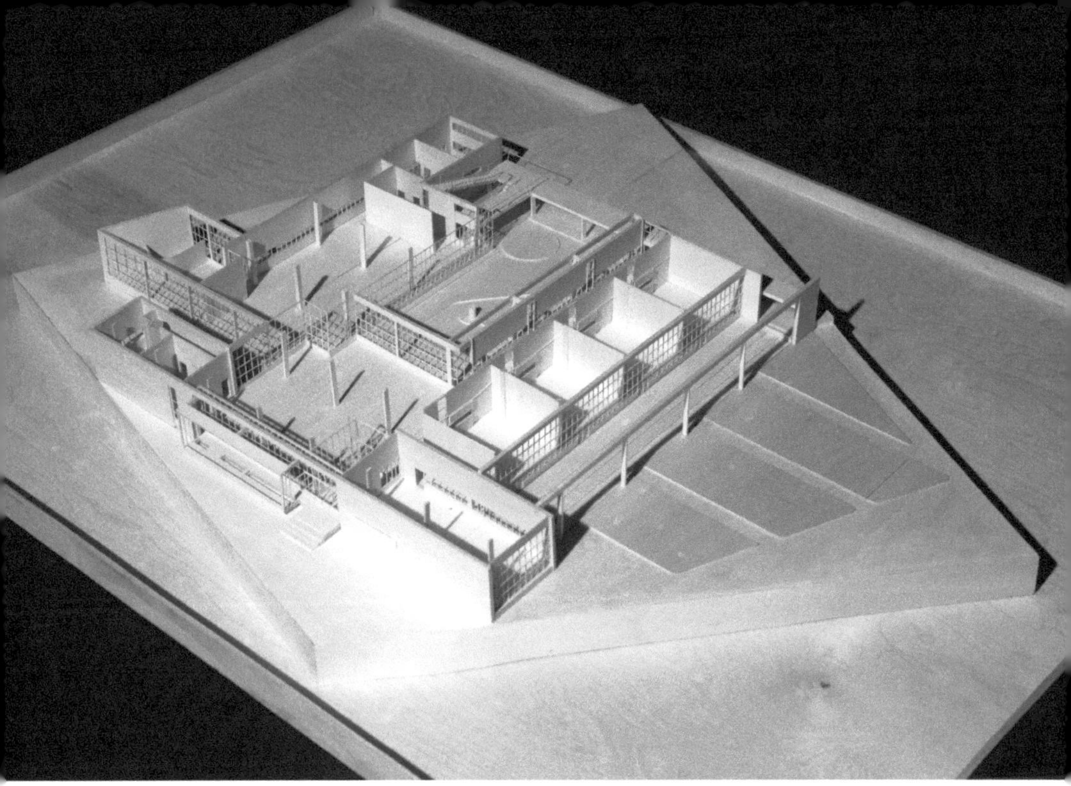

Image 16: Model of the Asilo from the Southeast

Image 17: Model of the Asilo from the Southwest

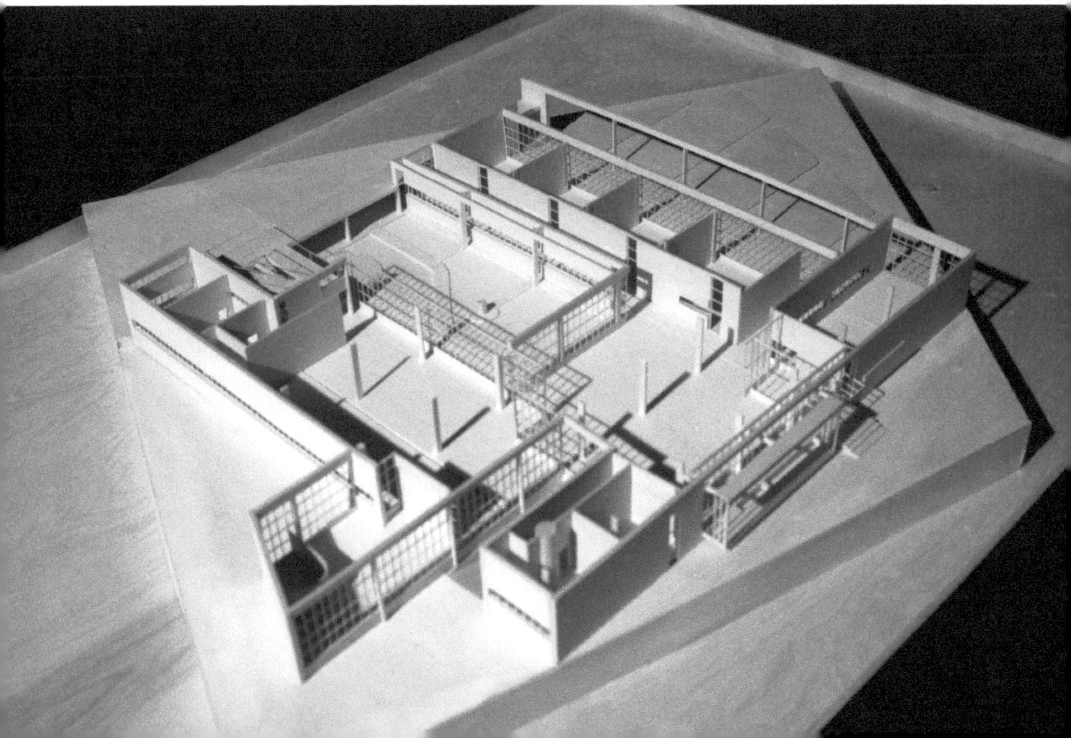

Image 18: Model of the Asilo from the South

Image 19: Model of the Asilo from the Northeast

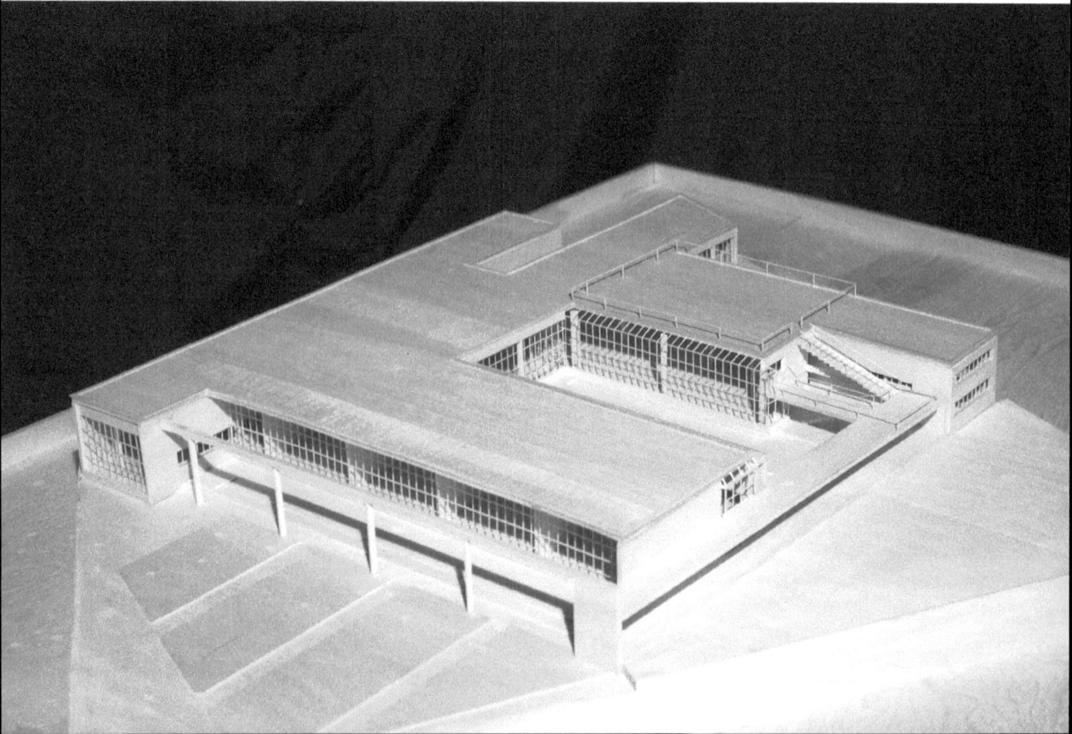

Image 20: Model of the Asilo from the Northwest

Image 21: Model of the Asilo from the Southwest

Image 22: Model of the Asilo from the Southeast

Image 23: Model of the Asilo, detail >

Bibliography

Thomas L. Schumacher, *Giuseppe Terragni: Surface and Symbol* (New York: Princeton Architectural Press, 1991)

Thomas L. Schumacher, *Global Architecture 74: Giuseppe Terragni* (Tokyo: ADA Edita, 1994) 2-47

Panos Koulermos, *20th Century European Rationalism* (London: Academy Group Ltd., 1995) 84-95

Attilio Terragni, Daniel Libeskind, and Paulo Roselli, *The Terragni Atlas: Built Architecture* (Milan: Skira, 2004) 22-117

Luigi Cavadini, *Il Razionalismo Lariano Como, 1926-1944* (Milan: Electa, 1989) 38-53, 70-79, 104-107

Enrico Mantero and Massimo Novati, *Il Razionalism Italiano* (Bologna: Zanichelli Editore, 1984) 89-91, 98-99, 160-167

Enzo Pifferi, *Giuseppe Terragni: Architetto Razionalista* (Como: Break Point, 2003) 4-61

Alessandra Coppa, Terragni: *E Il Razionalismo Lariano* (Como: Fondazione Cariplo, 2004) 4-37

Le Corbusier, *Vers Une Architecture* (Paris: G. Cres, 1924)193-212

Peter Eisenman, *Giuseppe Terragni: Transformations, Decompositions, Critiques* (New York: Monacelli Press, 2003

Giorgio Ciucci, *Giuseppe Terragni: Opera Completa* (Milan: Electa, 1996)

Massimo Bontempelli and P.M. Bardi, *Quadrante 35: Documentario Sulla Casa Del Fascio Di Como* (Como: Tipografia Editrice Cesare Nani, 1989)

Giovanna D'Amia, *Giuseppe Terragni: Oltre Il Razionalismo* (Como: Enzo Pifferi, 2003)

Thomas L. Schumacher, *The Danteum* (New York: Princeton Architectural Press, 1985

L. Ferrario and D. Pastore, *Giuseppe Terragni: La Casa Del Fascio* (Rome: Instituto Mides, 1982)

www.ingramcontent.com/pod-product-compliance
Lightning Source LLC
Chambersburg PA
CBHW040440190426
43202CB00034B/19